T-REXES vs KANGAROOS

AND OTHER STORIES

PRINTED BY CREATESPACE,
AN AMAZON.COM COMPANY

T-Rexes vs Kangaroos: And Other Stories
© 2015 Donor Relations Guru, LLC

ISBN 978-0-692525-75-3

Cover Design: Tyler Wessel Design
Interior Design: Tyler Wessel Design
Primary Author: Lynne M. Wester
Content Contributor: Debbie Meyers
Editor: Tyler Wessel (Tyler Wessel Design)

Printed by CreateSpace, An Amazon.com Company

For permission requests, please contact:

Lynne Wester
Donor Relations Guru, LLC
Lynne@DonorRelationsGuru.com

For design inquiries, please contact:

Tyler Wessel
Tyler Wessel Design
TLWessel@gmail.com

T-REXES vs KANGAROOS

IMPROVING YOUR FUNDRAISING AND DONOR RELATIONS

LYNNE M. WESTER
DONOR RELATIONS GURU

WITH CONTRIBUTIONS FROM DEBBIE MEYERS

TABLE OF CONTENTS

introduction

philosophical musings on fundraising

the donor relations profession

the practice of donor relations

unique donor populations

professional skills and management

appendix

A BRAIN LIKE
A BLOW TORCH

Gratitude unlocks the fullness of life. It turns what we have into enough, and more. It turns denial into acceptance, chaos into order, confusion to clarity. It can turn a meal into a feast, a house into a home, a stranger into a friend.

– Melody Beattie

As I thought about what would be my follow-up to my first book *The Four Pillars of Donor Relations*, I thought about you, the reader, and what you would like most.

I also thought about the wealth of information I had already shared with many of you for the past five years on my blog. As I began to look back over the posts, I began to look at them in terms of parts of a whole. I also laughed at how over the years my writing style has evolved.

I am blessed to share my blog in an edited and revised context with you here. My hope is that you will use it to have some thought-provoking conversations with yourself and others and also to take these practical tips and apply them in your every day work. May it be half the blessing for you in your work as it has been for me over the years.

I also hope for you that you sense the deep level of sarcasm and wit contained within. For me, there is no life without laughter.

> *I love people who make me laugh. I honestly think it's the thing I like most, to laugh. It cures a multitude of ills. Its probably the most important thing in a person.*
>
> *– Audrey Hepburn*

I give gratitude first and foremost to my parents, without which I would never be the woman I am today. Some people's cup of tea, a strong brew for sure, but I sure am a glad to be a good shot of Tequila for many. Or as a friend and client once told me, "Some people's brains work like a crock pot, some like a microwave, but yours my dear, is all blow torch! "

Thank you to my professional colleagues and mentors, without whom I am unable to grow. Additional gratitude goes to Debbie Meyers to her countless great additions to the chapters of this manuscript. To Mary, Tyler, Ashley, Nick, Nikki, Sarah, Jenny, Angie, Maureen, Matthew, Erin, Meghan, Gwen, and the countless others who help keep the DRG ship afloat and bring the waves ashore, my horizon of gratitude is without sunset.

> *As we express our gratitude, we must never forget that the highest appreciation is not to utter words, but to live by them.*
>
> *– John F. Kennedy*

PART 1

PHILOSOPHICAL MUSINGS ON FUNDRAISING

T-REXES vs KANGAROOS

FINDING A SHARED COMMONALITY

One of the challenges I often see in our organizations is the diversity of our fundraising workforce. Nope, I'm not talking about the fact that we as an industry lack ethnic and socioeconomic diversity in spade (more on that in a later chapter). I'm talking about the never ending struggle between two groups.

Now you're going to have to have a good sense of humor – and a vivid imagination – to make it through this book.

Picture this if you will: These are two opposing forces at work in our fundraising profession. (*Disclaimer: Help me out here by not focusing on the fact that these can be sweeping generalizations and are not true of everyone.*)

We have the **T-REXES**, wonderful people who have worked in our organizations for a long time (hence the pre-historic bend) and who are generally adverse to change. When a new idea comes, they use their ferocious growl and their short arms to try and bat new ideas down.

Then you have the **KANGAROOS**, (*note: not the job hoppers*). They've only been at the organization for a while, have worked at other non-profits and come bouncing in with a pouch full of new ideas and limitless energy. They annoy the heck out of the T-Rexes, who have seen them bounce in and out and around...and the T-Rexes are still there, regardless.

Have you ever seen a kangaroo fight? They're good at it! And, wow at the persistence (this is a Google and Youtube moment here)! But everyone is so scared of the T-Rex that they won't even attempt it. And this, my friends, is one of the reasons why our organizations cannot be innovative.

How do we soothe the fears of the T-Rexes and allow the kangaroos to adapt to the culture of the organization without each of them wishing the other extinct? How do we ensure that our culture doesn't run the kangaroo off? (Remember the average tenure of a front line fundraiser is 16 months right now). How do we get each of them to extend their short little arms for an HR-appropriate embrace?

The answer is that we must allow each person to understand that, whether they hop around the office or stomp around the office, **the relationship that matters the most is the one we have with our donors**. They are the center of our universe, whether it be a pre-historic swamp, or a grassland down unda.'

If we keep our mission and the donor at the center, then the length and effectiveness of our arms matters not. Our eons-long divide shortens and we focus on what truly matters, the wonderful experience of philanthropy. Because for all the differences between a T-Rex and a Kangaroo, they share a world view that philanthropy matters.

And when we point out that shared commonality, the differences begin to fade.

EVERYONE MUST BELIEVE

DONOR FOCUS STARTS AT THE TOP

The moment you doubt whether you can fly, you cease for ever to be able to do it.

– J.M. Barrie, *Peter Pan*

I'm here in Anaheim California and I thought that this quote would be a great beginning to a post about how donor relations truly works best in an organization.

I think it is essential, inextricable, vital that the donor focus start at the top. Not at the top of the donor pyramid, but at the top of the leadership pyramid of your organization. In order to revolutionize your organization's relationship with donors, the top must believe, and then you can fly.

I often come into organizations where someone along the great food chain has bought into the idea of donor relations and realizes the success they can have by forming proper donor relationships and putting donors at the center of what they do.The crucial point of the visit usually occurs when I meet the person in charge of the organization and ask their opinion on what it would be like to have ideal donor relations.

If their eyes twinkle and the words, "It's not just the right thing to do, it's a privilege," come flowing freely, then I know we can go far. If they hesitate and hem and haw about process and procedure and the importance of "getting dollars in the door," then I know we have a bumpy road to travel.

You see, the mindset must be part of a culture.

And more than a culture of philanthropy, a wonderful organization must have what I call an "attitude of gratitude". And folks, that starts at the top.

Leaders who are willing to throw themselves into thanking donors, even those who haven't given millions, inspire me. What they get out of it is multiplied. They see first hand that the simple act of gratitude can change their outlook, inspire good will and give them a glimpse into a philanthropist's heart. I am thrilled to say that these leaders far outnumber those who say, "I'll hire someone to do that touchy feely stuff."

So what's your goal? Maybe one of them should be to assess the culture of gratitude at your organization. Find out if people begrudgingly write thank you notes or if it's something they enjoy. It will tell you a great deal about where you're headed and how. I look to partner with people who "get it" and understand that gratitude is one of the best parts of our job.

People often ask me how to know if someone will be a good fit for donor relations if they have no prior experience. I tell them easily, if the person has gratitude in their heart and is quick to express it, that is someone I want talking to donors.

That's someone who believes.

IN DESPERATE NEED: TRANSLATORS

COMMUNICATIONS BETWEEN FUNDRAISERS AND THE DATA TEAM

As an undergraduate at the University of South Carolina (*Go Gamecocks!*) my first major was genetic engineering. After discovering that Calculus 4 and the laboratory life weren't for me, I changed my majors to foreign languages, with the goal to one day be an international translator.

Well, although I don't do that for a living, my translational skills are not lost, nor do they go unused on a daily basis. I find that one of the most essential positions for fundraising success is someone who can translate the communications between fundraisers and those that help make them successful.

I'm talking reporting, advancement services, donor relations, research etc. I think there is a fundamental difference in the way these two groups of people talk about donors, data, and its impact on fundraising for the organization.

Let's take a look at this relationship and communication dynamic. Paint with a wide brush with me and allow me some grace here. **Fundraisers**, for the most part, are *extroverts*. They build relationships and work in the cerebral space of relationships. Our **data folks,** by contrast, are *introverts* by nature. They work in the process oriented space and the cerebral space of data's impact on the greater picture.

Often times, fundraisers struggle with the ability to communicate to the data folks *what* they need and *why* they need it. Data folks are concerned with outcome of the data and ensuring that its value is not underestimated. Thus, the role of the divisional translator becomes inextricable from the operation, someone who can understand the delicacies of fundraising and, as I say, "speak geek" and understand data.

This is an art and a science and can be found in folks in all types of roles. I'm a hidden data nerd. Data drives everything I do and informs many decisions for me. It is helpful that in alumni and donor relations I can balance the relationships with the data.

Here are some tips I have learned to help the translators:

- Find a common vocabulary and set of definitions. What is a non-donor to one person is not to others. This is *essential*.

- Explain the use of the data and the need for it. *Why* do you want the report and *how* will it be used once provided?

- Appreciate that data doesn't just arrive at your feet. It takes work, time, and effort, just like cultivating a gift does, and sometimes just a long.

- Understand that both individuals have unique skill sets and that is okay. A database manager may shudder at the thought of asking someone for money and a fundraiser may get nauseous at the site of a query.

- Work together for the common good and try to find points of mutual understanding in order to better serve the one population we all share: donors.

GENEROSITY vs PHILANTHROPY

TRANSFORMING YOUR THINKING

Close your eyes. No peeking. *Though now I'm not sure how you'll keep on reading...*but I digress. Now, imagine for a moment the person that comes to the top of your mind when I say the word "philanthropist." Got them? Good.

Cement that image right there. Now play along again, close your eyes, and imagine the person that comes to the top of your mind when I say the word, "generous." No peeking! I'm a betting woman, so I'm going to bet that the two people you pictured were different individuals.

And that's exactly my point today. In our business of fundraising, we celebrate and laud the philanthropist. How many of us in our lifetimes will ever become philanthropists in the classic definition? Well, the first strike against us is that we work in the non-profit sector, so based on salary alone, probably not many. But most, if not all, of us are generous.

This community is one of the most giving, caring sectors out there. We are generous in many ways, with time, resources, advice, and monetarily. So what kind of message are we sending to our donors when we consistently promote philanthropy and what we really mean is generosity? I'm consistently asked how to recognize volunteers, not just donors. What if we recognized generosity instead?

Yup, I'm asking us to make another shift in the way we think. I've brought you along a journey where I avow that the thank is more important than the ask. Now I'm asking you to re-frame your thoughts around what it truly means to give.

I'm not saying that philanthropy and generosity are mutually exclusive. They're not. But the two words evoke completely different connotations. Remember, words matter to our supporters. Transforming your thinking can have wonderful engagement opportunities.

AN ATTITUDE OF GRATITUDE

WHY THE THANK YOU NOTE IS SO SPECIAL

I often stand in front of a room of people who know that donor relations is the right thing to do for their organization. They know that the investment is a worthwhile one. More and more, donor relations is becoming a mainstream core of effective and sophisticated fundraising efforts. Donor relations is not expensive, but neglecting it can be.

It doesn't take a great deal of money to have gratitude be pervasive in an organization's culture. We know it costs 7 times more to acquire a new donor than it does to keep the one you have. But it takes time and thought, and it requires a re-prioritization of our efforts. I often start my clients on simple journeys of gratitude to show the power and effectiveness of an *attitude of gratitude*.

Sometimes, we see gratitude come full circle on a national stage. Jordan Spieth became the second youngest person ever to win the Masters Golf Tournament. Soon after, his note of thanks for his high school scholarship became public on social media. In it, he mentions his dream of winning the Masters. He also expresses his genuine gratitude to his donors. I am sure they were proud then, and I'm sure they swell with pride now. This note alone is another reinforcement of why it is so important for us to encourage others to express their gratitude.

When I survey donors, time and time again, the one thing they want – **8 times more than any other donor relations communication** – is a thank you note from the recipient of their generosity. We can do this each and every time if we try. If we can't have the note come from the direct recipient, we can have one from their family or their community. We could also have one from a board member or a volunteer.

I believe it is essential to begin every board meeting by having all board members write 5 handwritten thank you notes to donors. It instills a culture of gratitude and helps retention greatly. It also shows board members that, for those who don't want to ask for money, thanking donors for their generosity is just as, if not more, important. Do you have your board members do this? It's a great activity for all involved.

Want a great gift to help people understand the power of gratitude, try the book, *With Gratitude* from my friend Jennifer Richwine. It's powerful and a wonderful guide on why the thank you note is so special and how to write one effectively and beautifully.

I look for this when hiring people in our profession, too. I often ask the last time they wrote a hand written thank you note. If they give me a blank stare and fumble, I know this isn't my hire. If they tell me in detail about a note they recently wrote, that's a good sign.

THE 58.9%

WHY DONORS STOP GIVING
TO AN ORGANIZATION

What is the number one factor why donors stop giving to an organization?

Too Frequent Solicitation/Asked for Inappropriate Amount: 58.9%

If you read the report on High Net Worth Donors every two years, the data enclosed is priceless. As I prowled through the 70 or so pages on my subway commute home from work, I read and reread the statistics, but one of them was just too powerful to shake from my consciousness.

Finding out why the majority of these donors stopped giving to an organization was enlightening and confirmed for me a long held belief of most organizations. We poke and prod our donors to give way too much. This is detrimental to our relationships with our donors and, as a result, to our bottom lines.

At many organizations, I have been responsible for drafting communications of all types to donors. Some are aimed to inform, some to steward, some to simply say hello. Always – and I do mean always – I have to fend off an over eager or confused annual giving or major giving officer and say, "No, we don't need to ask them for another gift in this piece."

Sometimes it is a losing battle, but every time I have and will fight for a solicitation-free space.

I hope now, thanks to studies like this and others, that this battle is much easier fought and won at my organizations. Fingers crossed and hoping for myself and others,

Some might say, "Well, if we don't ask often enough they will forget to give to us!" This may be a valid argument, but what would happen if we asked less and communicated in a more engaging and enlightening way? I am sure these educated adults will figure out how to give, perhaps on our website with its glowing gold "DONATE NOW" button the size of Texas on our homepage.

I say this with my tongue firmly implanted in my cheek. However, in reality, I am a strong advocate for communications that do just that: communicate for the relationship's sake. If we do that effectively, the money will follow.

ADDRESS LABELS. REALLY?

SOLICITATIONS: THE GOOD, BUT MOSTLY THE UGLY

I recently received two mail solicitations from two completely different organizations.

One was from a national cancer charity and one was from a former employer. What is so enlightening and thought-provoking is just how off-base both of them were! It truly demonstrated to me that solicitations, just like donor relations, needs to be thoughtful, purposeful, and relevant to the audience.

Let's examine them both as case studies.

First I received what we will call the "mid-level" solicitation. As all of you know, I have been studying, writing, and presenting on mid-level donors a great deal lately and even wrote on the subject a while back. This was a form letter – addressed properly, at least – that was "written" by a student. In it, I was asked to make a $1,885/year commitment for 4 years. A solid mid-level ask and a commitment, considering my last and largest gift to them was $150 when I was still employed there.

This letter was impersonal, unattached and clearly was pulled off of some sort of LYBUNT or SYBUNT list. On the back of the letter they had printed an "Honor Roll of Donors" of those who had joined this giving society by making this particular commitment of which they were asking of me.

I was instantaneously turned off. Reasons why as follows:

1. The letter was impersonal and seemingly came out of "nowhere." I haven't received an email, no invitations, nothing – except this ask – in a long while!

2. That level of ask shouldn't come through a letter, in my opinion. I mean, can I get a phone call, a visit, – something! – before you ask me for the equivalent of $7,500?

3. Listing others who have given at that level does nothing for me, except make me think that they have plenty of donors at this already, including all of the trustees, so why do they need me?

4. If they had engaged me digitally, or at all, to gauge my interests and learn more about me as a donor and person before sending this blind solicitations, I might have been more receptive.

Needless to say, I won't be joining the cause.

Second, I received a really pretty envelope from a national cancer charity and instantly I saw the address labels peeking out from inside. Sigh. Address labels...really? Inside was a letter and flyers for how I could buy magazine subscriptions for $10 a piece and support their cause.

Again, I was instantly turned off, here's why:

1. Again, address labels...really? I pay my bills online, and rarely do I need my return address, if I do I just write it in. Jeesh! How old fashioned!

2. How "ungreen" of them! Think of the thousands of these they mailed out wasting paper and money.

3. Could you please solicit me by email or online? That is the way I live, and if you knew that, you would never mail to me.

4. Ordering magazines? I mean, really? Seriously? I am philanthropic to a cause, to support something I believe in, not to get discounted magazines. And did I mention that I read most of my magazines online now?

So now that I've complained sufficiently and told you why I won't be giving to these two, let me tell you about a wonderful solicitation I received. One of my friends is doing a walk for the March of Dimes. I received a personal email from an old college buddy (and Facebook friend), including a video pulling at my heartstrings. He told us in that email why he is walking.

Did I give? Absolutely. For many reasons:

1. It was digital. Lord knows he didn't send me a letter! It was multimedia, including a video!

2. It was personal, directed at me...

3. I already had a relationship with this person and this isn't the only time he talks to me.

4. I felt connected to his story and understood why it meant a great deal to my friend.

5. I knew my money was needed and wasn't wasted on superfluous things like address labels!

SILVER SURFERS

GENERATIONAL MYTHS AND OTHER FUNDRAISING UNTRUTHS

On this episode of Fundraising Mythbusters, we're going to tackle some commonly held falsehoods. Buckle up for the ride folks and be ready for some of your commonly held beliefs to be challenged.

MYTH 1: OLDER DONORS AREN'T TECH SAVVY

This is probably the myth I am most presented with on a daily basis as a challenge to my new ideas regarding technology. It's simply not true.

The baby boomer generation has now turned into a new catch phrase called the "Silver Surfers." They are retired and have dispensable time and income, they want badly to keep up with the younger folks, and technology is the great equalizer.

My parents, both part of the Silver Surfer generation, have separate laptops, a smart phone, and pay all of their bills online. They aren't the exception, they're the norm.

The #1 growing group on social media is women 55 and older, and the majority of new users for Skype is older gentlemen (65-plus). Online shopping has boomed and there is no excuse why digital media and your use of it shouldn't accommodate these folks. That doesn't mean that hand written notes should fall by the wayside – they are still tops – but don't eliminate digital ideas or let someone deter you because the "older" folks don't "do" technology.

MYTH 2: MEMBERS OF GENERATION X AREN'T GOOD GIVERS AND AREN'T ENGAGED

You know, the classes of the 80s and 90s that you struggle with? Those in their late 30s or 40s? They're out there and they're engaged, they're just *busy* and you aren't connecting with them yet in a meaningful manner.

My brother is one of those people, and I have to say that, of his three alma maters, only one does it somewhat well. The others have not connected. Yet.

This generation is building their careers and families; their time is short and valuable. Do you have folks on Wall Street? Don't call them once the bell has rung; you're costing them money. Send them a LinkedIn email or find another way to reach out; they will appreciate your awareness. Events don't work for these folks unless there's something in it for them. Adapt your style to fit them.

MYTH 3: RECENT COLLEGE GRADUATES – ALSO KNOWN AS THE MILLENNIAL GENERATION – DON'T CARE AND DON'T RESPOND

Not true. This generation understands philanthropy well, they jut don't understand old-school development operations well. You're not going to appeal to them with a phonathon; this is the generation of Toms shoes and the RED campaign, where products include philanthropy and their time is part of their philanthropy.

How do we convert them from giving their time to giving their money? We explain it to them, show the impact of the dollar, have peers tell the story, and allow them to have hands-on experiences that make a difference.

This generation has been wired since they were born, but unplugging them and having face-to-face time is vital to your success with this group. Show them the impact of a hand written note, and take the time to teach them how to write them; they probably were never taught.

Trying to reach them? Send them a text, reach out through social media; remember, with these folks email is waning. Send them a mobile call-to-action or involve them in a blitz fundraising campaign.

And do me a favor, stop calling them Young Alumni; not all of them were 21 when they graduated. Call them Recent Graduates or some other name, stop reminding them they're young. You don't remind your older donors they're old all the time do you?

MYTH 4: IF A NEW EFFORT FAILS, THROW IT OUT AND PRETEND IT NEVER HAPPENED

Learn from it, celebrate your failure, and instead of completely ridding yourself of the memory, try to find tweaks to help manage your challenges. Every problem has a solution, one that takes an excellent idea and impeccable implementation. Which one of these was your downfall?

These are the things that keep me up at night, filled with delight of solving, I love a challenge. What caused the unexpected success? What led to the downfall? What could we have done better? Can I build a better implementation plan to make it smoother, better, easier, faster? Is there technology that can match my weaknesses? These are the things we have to think about, instead of just dismissing it as a waste of time.

MYTH 5: TODAY'S TECHNOLOGY IS EXPENSIVE AND PROHIBITIVE

As technology evolves, the cost begins to plummet. Remember the $600 VCRs? The first bag phones? Exactly. (Admit it, some of you have no idea what I'm talking about).

Most technology is free or cheap to implement and has a relatively short time commitment to learn. Technophobe? No worries, find someone who is a wiz and have them help you.

When I first started speaking, I hated PowerPoint, so I had my work-study students help me build my presentations. Now I can crank out a great slide deck in under 15 minutes. I spend a great deal of time in Excel, but for the life of me can't make it print pretty – all on one page with headings and a readable font – for meetings. No worries, I have a friend on staff that makes me look great. It takes her less than ten minutes to do what it would take me two hours and lots of paper to do.

The trick is finding a solution around your barriers with technology. Don't have the budget to do that thank you video? Have a student video contest and...wham! Multiple great videos are created and students are better educated about philanthropy.

THE SUBJECT LINE

TIPS ON GETTING BETTER OPEN RATES

It's something I hear all the time:

No one opens our emails, how do we fix it?

I have a fantastic open and click-through rate for our donor relations emails; it hovers in the 40 percent range consistently. The average non-profit gets 15-20 percent. So here's the key: it's all about those 5 or so words you place in the subject line. Here are some tips:

IT'S NOT ABOUT YOU, SILLY!

A subject line should be centered around the donor, not you. An example: *The President and trustees of XYZ invite you to join them...*

A better option: *You are invited to join...* Notice the switch in subject. It is imperative that our communications are about the donor first, us second.

KEEP IT TRANSPARENT.

Let them know why you are writing. If it's an invitation, it should say so; a holiday greeting, an ask, etc. One of the ways to do this is to send from different email aliases, donorrelations@, giving@, alumni@, etc. But also understand that if you're trying to "hide" an ask in an email, people will be perturbed by the supposed trickeroo.

KEEP IT CONSISTENT.

For every piece, do you have a plan for follow up, etc? Here is an example: for each event we have emails that go out, in a precise order, always the same so the recipient knows what to expect: save the date, invitation, reminder, reminder, follow-up for both attendees and non-attendees, without exception. Having this built in advance saves us from scrambling and creates a consistent message.

CALL THEM TO ACTION!

Most people see emails as an electronic to-do list, so give them something to do. This means that in your subject lines, avoid any form of the verb "to be" and use active verbs: join, help, empower, support, learn, respond, etc...

USE A/B TESTING

You'll need to do some testing to see what your group responds to. We call it A/B testing. Thinking of new subject lines? Great, now take half of your list and send them one, and send the other half another and see which one outperforms the other. This testing will help you hone in on effective keywords for your population.

TELL YOUR STORY

Examine the emails you receive from organization;, which ones do you open? The one that says: "Monthly XYZ newsletter" or one that says "Learn how XYZ changed Johnny's life!" Remember, a powerful story is important for your messaging and carries many times more of an impact than stats and figures.

AVOID SHOWCASING YOUR ADMINISTRATION/STAFF

Instead, showcase those that benefit from support. This is especially important for annual and mid-level donors. They don't relate to Dean So-and-So or CEO or Vice President; those aren't the people they give to. They give to sick children, college students, researchers, and other beneficiaries. Avoid titles and figureheads unless it's a communication that can come from only them.

TOUCHING A NERVE

LACK OF DIVERSITY IN
THE FUNDRAISING PROFESSION

Okay, so this one is probably going to get me into some trouble. But hey, when have I ever shied away from being controversial? With all that has been happening now across America and with all that I have seen and experienced, I wouldn't be true to myself if I didn't write this post.

As I travel all across this land, and sometimes even north of the border, I am constantly disappointed by the lack of diversity in the room. I'm not just talking ethnic diversity, I'm also talking religious, sexual orientation, and socio-economic diversity.

We are not doing a great job as leaders representing our constituencies.

The faces are mostly white, mostly upper middle-class, and the people we are raising funds for are certainly not. And don't get me started on what our volunteer boards look like!

In the field of donor relations, it's even worse; we're 90 percent white females. We represent institutions of higher learning, non-profits that help change the state of poverty, hospitals who cure illnesses, and yet I believe we have a problem within. One would think that higher education would be a wonderful place to promote diversity and inclusion, but when looking further, if we consistently refuse to change our own processes and avoid progress in our methodologies to fund raise, how can we expect to change the recruitment of diverse populations of professionals?

We don't actively recruit and mentor people who don't even know that fundraising is a career possibility. There is, in fact, an active glass ceiling in fundraising for some as well. We need to reach out to people and educate then on what a fabulous career this is and how they can become involved. That means reaching out to people who are not currently connected with or employed by a non-profit organization, but who are seeking to enter the profession or change careers. This also means being comfortable with having uncomfortable discussions on issues surrounding race, religion, and socioeconomic status.

Embracing diversity means having a genuine respect for differing perspectives – regardless whether you agree with every single thing about them – so that solutions encompass all diverse views and needs. Diversity increases the wealth of knowledge and ideas available, as long as they all look for creative and mutually satisfactory solutions.

We must be committed to inclusion ourselves and make our profession attractive to those who have not previously been exposed to it. It takes commitment to move the needle. We must be concerned with how to keep diversity/inclusion at the forefront of people's consciousness, and not be seen in a negative light. This requires systematic change, embedded in everything we do.

I have seen many examples of language or communications where, if a diverse eye were directed toward the content, it would have been significantly altered. For those of you reading this and feeling uncomfortable...good, mission accomplished. For those of you nodding heads and actively sharing this post with others, what's the next step?

First, be aware of the problem, then action and activity. I think many of us are aware of the problem, but have not yet taken concerted action. I approach this subject knowing it will raise eyebrows with some and elicit eyerolls from others. I'm determined to share my vocation with others; it's a wonderful profession.

STOP THE MADNESS!

TROUBLING NUMBERS REGARDING DIRECT MAIL

Over the past 6 months, I have been keeping a box of the direct mail solicitations that come to me here in Charlotte. After 6 months of diligence, I have some startling results to report to you. I began with a shoebox and ended up with a postal service tub of mail.

My hope is that you share this chapter with everyone you know in the hopes that behaviors will change.

It seems that direct mail is alive at some organizations, although the ROI on direct mail continues to fall. Remember, it is 7 times more expensive to obtain a new donor than it is to keep the one you already have. Adjust 10% of your acquisition budget into donor relations to boost retention and you won't regret the decision!

Over the 6 months I collected these mailings, I received 81 direct mail solicitations. Here is how they break down:

- 19 of those appeals were from organizations that I had *never* supported before, meaning they bought my name from a list clearinghouse or another organization. This frustrates me beyond repair, especially since it is in such direct violation of the Donor Bill of Rights.

- I received 53 solicitations in the dreaded and boring #10 envelope

- 18 solicitations were in non-standard sized envelopes.

- 45 of my solicitations came in window envelopes.

- 4 had errors in spelling of my name or address.

- 6 of the appeals claimed to have "emergency" or "urgent" appeals enclosed.

- I was sent 26 solicitations with free gifts enclosed, from notepads to Christ medals to calendars to 15 pages of address labels in all shapes and sizes. SIGH.

- 26 were sent with live stamps.

- 55 used non-profit postage bulk mail.

Let's look at the contents:

- 23 letters addressed me as "friend" or didn't use my name even though it was on the outer envelope. Do they just not care?

- 27 used my formal name of Ms. Wester.

- 18 of them used my first name of Lynne.

- And 11 used the weird combo of first and last name- which read, "Dear Lynne Wester."

The letters varied in length:

- 17 one page letters

- 47 two page letters

- 15 four or more page letters, with the longest being 8 pages. WOW.

67 of their appeals asked for a specific amount; 14 did not.

On the reply devices, only 6 – six! – offered me a monthly giving option.

I made a gift to one well-known national organization – by FAR the worst offender in address labels – and in order to thank me, they RE-SOLICITED ME! Also, on the thank you note, they referred to me as "friend." I won't be giving to them again.

So what have we learned from all of this?

It is that the status quo is in full effect at organizations. 81 pieces of mail later and I wasn't truly inspired by any of them. How are we going to cause change to happen in our organizations when we accept this as the norm?

I ask you to help me stop the madness! We *can* do better and we *must* do better!

SILOS ARE FOR GRAIN

NOT FUNDRAISING AND DONORS

One of the greatest obstacles my clients have to overcome is the behavior and activity surrounding silos. Remember, silos don't just house grain, they're often used for missiles. And that leads to destruction. Housing your fundraising and donors in silos will also lead to destruction.

Siloed behavior seems to happen without regard to the size of the organization. It is true that large fundraising teams who are decentralized can have more occurrences of this poor behavior because of their nature and structure, but I often see this even in small shops of less than 30 people.

What does siloed behavior look like in fundraising? Let me give you some examples:

- Alumni offices declaring that they "don't fund raise" and don't integrate with annual giving.

- Annual giving and major gifts not collaborating together to share donors.

- Thinking about communicating to donors and saying, "We need to add an email to this effort."

- Bringing in donor relations and stewardship after a major gift is closed...sigh.

- Not involving research professionals in discussions about our constituents.

- Changing a giving reply device without coordinating the impact of the change with gift processing staff.

- Holding onto donor contact information and not recording it in the database or keeping a separate list outside of the database.

- Anytime a staff member says, "Those are my donors, I would rather you not contact them."

- Thinking that social media is an afterthought to a communications plan.

I could go on for days, but at every turn, behaviors and silos don't benefit anyone.

I often speak with donors who don't understand that our organizations are large complex behemoths of bureaucracy and hierarchy; nor should they have to. Some donors are under the impression that I actually know who the bursar is, not to mention having breakfast with him or her daily. They don't need to know that we're decentralized. Our structure and lack of collaboration and seamless communication should never be a burden to them.

One of the things I really appreciate about my experience with my alma mater, South Carolina, is that I can go to my person with a question or request about almost anything and, rather than passing me off to someone or somewhere else, he finds the information out and helps me. It's seamless and efficient and provides for me a great service that helps me know they care.

This is all well and valid, but how do we break down silos so that our donors and our fundraising don't suffer?

- Realize and identify that silos actually exist in your organization.

- Once identified, examine how these affect your donors.

- Seek out leadership that encourages staff to collaborate.

- Identify opportunities for collaboration.

- Form cross silo task forces to tackle problems from a variety of viewpoints.

- Reward and incentivize collaborative behavior.

- Take deep breaths and understand that the only one who suffers in silos are the donors; we owe them better.

THE BIG "C"

CAMPAIGNS ARE NOT JUST ABOUT REACHING THE GOAL

It seems like the "C" word is everywhere all the time. That's *Campaigns* for those of you who are confused.

For many of us, in regards to a comprehensive campaign, we're either in one, around one, or on one. The business of fundraising always seems like the business of campaigns. I'm not sure they're always necessary, but our boards and leaders seem to love them.

So how many of you are around a campaign and what phase are you in? Do you have a comprehensive campaign plan for donor relations? If not, how do you plan on effective implementation?

So many times I receive calls from folks who say to me, "We're wrapping up a campaign, and now we need stewardship, what do we do?" Unfortunately, backpedaling and being campaign reactionary is often unsuccessful and appears haphazard. It also places a heavy burden on donor relations.

The best way to move through a campaign with donor relations is side-by-side with your feasibility study, campaign counsel, and in partnership with your leadership. You need to be there in the beginning so that you are consistently placing strategic donor relations at the center of every activity, from launch to closing. Again, it's about putting yourself in the conversations and showing the value of donor relations.

Oftentimes, consultants and leadership are too focused on the pursuit of major gifts and don't always have the perspective of the other parts of the giving cycle because they are keenly focused on reaching the goal. It's not just about reaching the goal; it's about what do we do to reward those who got us there and how do we think about the folks for the next campaign, **preparing them to feel amazing about their philanthropy.**

Part of our role is to share the attitude of gratitude with others, from volunteers to constituents to leadership. It starts with you. It starts with small steps that lead to huge success.

So here are some tangible action items:

- Perform an audit of your activities.

- Are they all best practices and benchmarked with peer organizations?

- Are all of your funds organized, properly spent and stewarded?

- Is your acknowledgment process efficient and sensible?

- If those foundational bedrocks aren't in place, how can you do other things?

DUDE, WHERE'S THE BATHROOM?

ONBOARDING NEW FUNDRAISING PROFESSIONALS

One of the things that fascinates me every time I start a new job is the onboarding process that the employer offers. By far and away the best employer I ever had at this was Walt Disney World. Ever since then, every university I've worked for hasn't done so great.

What is your on boarding process? I'm currently working with a client to help them develop their training programs for support staff and development officers. It's been fascinating. Here are some of my observations:

1. I don't need database training in my first week. I need someone to show me where the bathroom is and how to work my phone. Seriously.

2. In my first week, I want to be introduced to those that can best help me be successful. Give me time with them so I can learn what they do.

3. In my first week, give me a real life view of the organizational culture, explain to me the meetings that I might not know about.

4. In my first week, give me an entire half-day to figure out my office setup and get organized.

5. Pair me with someone who can help me navigate the channels of bureaucracy and be there to answer questions when I have them, no matter how large or small.

6. Have someone take me to lunch and explain the unwritten rules, pet peeves, and quirks of my new leadership so I don't "step in it" in my first month.

7. After I've settled in, *then* set me up with formal training. Give me a chance to have input in the order and intensity of those trainings. I may not need Excel 101 or to spend 3 hours learning how to use Outlook.

8. If you work in an area of particular interest, especially donor or alumni relations, become a part of orientation and meet with every new employee as a matter of course. Be a resource for them. Help them out when they wander the halls or need a good pen.

9. For all that is holy, if I've relocated to a new place, offer to help me locate simple services that make my life easier. Sometimes it's so awkward to ask. I've been so fortunate in my relocations to NYC and Charlotte that people helped me in innumerable ways. I've taken them up on their offers and it was amazingly helpful.

10. Invite me to more meetings than you think are necessary on order to find the landscape. Then after I attend a few, let me choose from there.

11. Finally, have a plan in place when someone arrives. Without a plan to follow through on all the details, I have a chance of seeming disoriented and lost.

REALLY OUTTA' WHACK

YOUR ASK-TO-THANK RATIO

So I'm an admitted fundraising nerd. That's okay, I tell myself all the time. I base many of my findings on data; I love data. Data doesn't lie and is difficult to dispute. I've been tracking some interesting data for the past 6 months and I have some findings to share with you.

It involves donor retention and the fact that our first time donors are leaving us in alarming amounts. Remember, according to the wonderful people at Bloomerang, first time donor retention hovers at 23 percent. When we ask donors why they don't give again, over-solicitation is the number one reason.

Well, I now have living proof of that.

I constantly ask non-profits for their ask-to-thank ratio. Not just hard asks, but those supposed "soft" asks too. Remember, there is NO such thing as a "soft" ask to a donor; that's like being "partially" pregnant. An ASK is an ASK.

Anyway, folks, it's really outta' whack.

I gave numerous gifts online on Giving Tuesday; here is my experience with a few nonprofits from the list. *Note that I have removed the organizations' names.*

ORGANIZATION A:

In six months, I've received 2 thank yous, and one receipt. So I'll count that at 3. Since December, I've received 19 solicitations. 3 in the postal mail, and 16 emails. 8 emails in December alone.

- Asks: 19, Thanks: 3
- Donor Retention: NOT LIKELY

ORGANIZATION B:

In six months, I've received 3 thank yous and one receipt. That's 4. I've also received one solicitation.

- Asks: 1, Thanks: 4
- Donor Retention: VERY LIKELY

ORGANIZATION C:

In six months, I've received a WHOPPING 44 solicitations: 40 emails, 4 in the postal mail. Compared to 2 thank yous, including the receipt. In December, after I made my gift on the 3rd, I received 23 ASKS IN DECEMBER ALONE.

- Asks: 44, Thanks: 2
- Donor Retention: SERIOUSLY?

The opposite is also true. I haven't heard from some of the organizations I gave to in December at all since the day I gave. Three organizations all sent thank yous the day I gave and have never once re-solicited me.

- Asks: 0, Thanks: 1
- Donor Retention: NOT LIKELY

Many of you are probably asking, what is the correct ask-to-thank ratio?

Unfortunately, I don't have a magic answer for you. I think it honestly depends on your donor base. But I can tell you the following: You can't ask again until you've properly thanked the donor and explained the impact of *their* gift. (See Charity Water for an example of this done correctly. Their ratio is 5 ASKS to 8 THANKS so far).

The first step is identifying your ask-to-thank ratio, not hard asks or soft ones but asks, period. In thanks, I'm generous here. You can count a receipt, an acknowledgment, and any impact or gratitude piece.

I'D RATHER BUY GOATS

ONLINE GIVING SITES:
IS YOURS DONOR FOCUSED?

How easy do you make it or your constituents to give to you online?

I'm not talking about your "give now" button or your homepage design, but rather the design of your actual giving page mechanism and the experience your donors have when attempting to make an online gift.

Seriously, I can buy a flock of goats on Amazon with a few clicks and get free 2-day shipping, but to give to some colleges requires me to click 70 times through a dozen pages.

Online giving is the fastest growing giving method, up 20% in the last year alone, as more and more people completely wire their lives and use mobile devices before desktop useage.

So I must ask you if you have looked at your online giving statistics lately? Do you know the percentage of your donors that give online? Have you tried making a gift online to your organization recently? Have you checked out your giving website on your smartphone? What is your abandon rate on your giving site? This means how many people click on your site, attempt to fill out your form and then leave without making a gift?

Part of the consulting work I do is to help people optimize their online giving and make it donor focused, so I have quite a list of questions I need to ask you:

THE SITE SHOULD NOT TAKE LONG TO COMPLETE.

If you make it long and cumbersome with many boxes, required info and such, you are killing your rates.

In addition, leave your development jargon off of this page. How do I know what a *constituent* means to you? And look at that scary drop-down of giving choices – what do they mean? And why is unrestricted *last*?

CAN I MAKE A PLEDGE AND PAY A PLEDGE ONLINE?

If not, why not? This should be easy! If I am allowed to pledge online, my gift will be larger!

Also, on one site I helped with there is a nifty campaign thermometer redesigned at the bottom and a link to a map so you can see where other donors are from. Interactive and brilliant!

IS THERE AN OPTION FOR MONTHLY GIVING?

I want to be able to give you my credit card number and have you deduct a certain amount each month on a date that I specify. These gifts are larger than one time gifts and allow you to have fewer lapsed donors. An option to be reminded of the payment by email is brilliant and donor friendly!

CAN I GIVE USING MY IPHONE, IPAD, AND ANDROID TO GIVE?

What does your site look like on a smaller screen? Remember, if you send me an email appeal and call-to- action, I will probably open it on my mobile device and act right away. If you make that difficult and I can't complete the transaction from my device, you've lost my money!

WHEN I COMPLETE GIVING, WHAT DO I SEE?

I should see an immediate acknowledgment and a page where I can share the news that I just made a gift to you via integrated Facebook, Twitter, and other links, so I can let others know! This is so easy to do its ridiculous but we still seem to be missing it!At the minimum, take me to a page where I can join your LinkedIn group, like your Facebook page, or follow you on Twitter!

If I just made a gift, I'm more likely to do so again!

AM I SENT AN EMAIL ACKNOWLEDGMENT AND RECEIPT IMMEDIATELY?

Save your paper here, folks! If I'm giving to you digitally, thank and receipt me in the same manner!

HOW MANY FIELDS DO I NEED TO FILL OUT?

As far as the actual payment, remember that I don't have to give you a blood sample and my first born child in order for you to process my credit card! The information can be minimal, especially once I give you my CVV code! Stop making me answer 60 questions just because you want more data!

IS IT EASY FOR ME TO DESIGNATE MY FUNDS?

Is there a box I can tell you more about where I want my money to go? Why do I have to search to find what you want me to give to? This is too much work for me to give YOU a GIFT!

DO YOU BOX IN MY GIVING?

For all that is good and holy, stop suggesting amounts to me with radio buttons! You've probably aimed too low or too high and I'm not happy about that. If I'm going online to give you $100 and you start your giving options with $25 what do you think I'm going to do?

THAT BEING SAID, PLEASE MAKE SURE I CAN GIVE YOU A LARGE AMOUNT ONLINE.

I may need some airline miles and paying my $50,000 pledge online will help me get elite status. I've seen it happen and I've seen organizations that won't let a donor give large gifts online, or limits the type of credit card I can use. Don't cut off American Express just because it costs more; it is my card of choice, especially for large gifts. If you stop me from using it, you are killing my donation amount – and your campaign numbers. And remember, most Amex's don't have limits!

FUNDRAISING AS A VOCATION, NOT A JOB

DOING WHAT YOU LOVE TO DO

There are two types of people that work in non-profit fundraising: those who have a job and those who have a vocation. Distinct and telling differences emerge when you examine those two types of people.

Many times I am often asked why I do all I do. My first answer usually revolves around insomnia; my second answer strikes at the core of who I am: fundraising is my passion. I fully feel that there are two types of people working in our field. Some who feel it is their day job and the rest of us that feel it is our vocation or calling.

Growing up, I was the kid who never knew what she wanted to be when she grew up. Among my lifelong dream careers were the first female NFL referee, the next Ernest Hemingway, and a restaurant critic. Never did I say I wanted to be a donor relations professional.

After trying many things from a boat captain to a pastry chef to a teacher and a bartender, when I found philanthropy, something in me changed. We now have the opportunity to teach others about our profession, to hire the kinds of people that inspire us to do better.

So why am I on this vocation kick? Because I meet people who are just in it for other reasons and I'm baffled. You won't become rich working in non-profit fundraising, but boy is your heart full.

The dictionary defines vocation as "a strong feeling of suitability for a particular career or occupation." The first time I heard vocation it was in 8th grade when I had to take a series of all of the vocations, including wood and metal shop, agriculture, home economics (am I dating myself?), typing, and auto shop. But I am now convinced more than ever that fundraising is my vocation. I chose higher education as my specialty for a deeply personal reason that I won't go into in this blog (let's just say it involves my Dad), but one day, if you catch me at a bar over a glass of Malbec, I'll try telling you without crying.

The folks I tend to do business with, those whom I admire, and those whom are my mentors all are in this profession and see it as their vocation. I actively choose not to spend my time on and with those who see it as another job or a means to an end. They exhaust me. As some might say, they don't "get it."

A job is defined as "the work that a person does regularly in order to earn money." This designates a few differentiations from a vocation. The first is that the end goal is money; anyone in non-profit will tell you the benefits are great, the pay is not that fabulous. The second thing about a job is that it seems to have a finite end and purpose. I just cannot say that about a vocation. My vocation consumes me at times, for better or worse.

Maybe I can relate it in philanthropic terms. People who work in non-profit fundraising as a vocation are donors, and those who see it as a job are non-donors. Is that too bold of a statement?

YOUR DATABASE ISN'T THE PROBLEM

IS YOUR DATA MISMANAGED?

There are few absolute truths in fundraising. No matter how large or small the organization, there are a few things I've never heard:

> *We have plenty of staff, time, money, and resources.*

> *Managing volunteers is easy.*

> *Our database is perfect and I get happy just logging in every day.*

After you've finished giggling, consider this thought: **the database isn't the problem**. The problem is the way it's managed, used, resourced, etc.

For the past 12 or so years, I've had great relationships with all of the major fundraising database providers, regardless of how many times they change their names or buy other companies. I'm a fan of Banner (gasp), I think Raiser's Edge is brilliant, and find that databases are not the Darth Vader we all make them out to be. However, as I have mentioned, I am a self-confessed data nerd as well.

So how do I help you stop banging your head on your desk and using your database's name as a four letter word?

It's simple, I'm going to help you make it easier for everyone.

The database shouldn't be blamed for the following:

- Its software hasn't been updated in years (think of not updating the apps on your phone).

- There is ONE person with the proper training to understand how it works.

- The database doesn't work like Amazon or Google.

- The people managing the database are never allowed out of their cubicles (which usually reside in basement, converted garage, or strip mall, far from the fancy corner offices some of us live in). No one ever invites the data folks to meetings. Think of all of the factors and ask yourselves if you would be high functioning if these circumstances were true.

Follow along a metaphor with me. Have you ever met someone who can understand and speak multiple languages? We all *need* to have someone like this in our organizations. Unfortunately, so much is lost in translation. We need to hire more people that understand fundraising but also "speak geek" as I say it (I address this earlier in an earlier chapter).

I happily serve as this translator at many organizations. How do we intelligently explain our needs to folks who have never met a donor in most cases? How do they build reports that work for fundraisers if they aren't included in the process from the beginning? We need to advocate for resources for the center, to build our infrastructure. I can tell you that good data folks will make you millions; bad data and poor infrastructure can ruin an operation. It's not the system, it's how it's used, managed and resourced. It takes time, dedication, and money to build a proper infrastructure, but it is a phenomenal investment.

How do we educate the non-believers? We show them that regardless of the database or system, if it's junk in, it's junk out. We tell them that they have to explain *why* they need the report and what they're going to do with it.

We also need to send data folks to fundraising conferences and fundraisers to database conferences. Spending a day in someone's shoes is a wonderful way to help them appreciate. Some folks don't know what the end user needs and why that makes sense. Finally, we need to hire people with multiple sets of skills and help designate the translators to bridge the gaps.

DEAR FUNDRAISER

AN OPEN LETTER FROM YOUR FRIEND IN DONOR RELATIONS

Pardon me for writing you a letter, I hope you'll read it and it will start a discussion between and among us. You see, I feel like we need to talk. I know, I know, you're off to visit a donor and don't have time, but read this on the plane on the way there.

First, I'm here to help. I want you to be a fundraising rock star. I want us to be a team.

I come from a place of yes, and I want others to as well. I'm excellent with details and rules and can navigate bureaucratic nightmares swiftly like a water moccasin. I'm a people pleaser who just needs a little positive affirmation and some team work, and wow, can I move mountains for you. I seem to be able to pull off the impossible and deliver it with a smile. Behind the scenes I'm sometimes exhausted and frustrated; it's just reality, but I sure do love what I do.

Here's where you can help me help you.

Put information in the database and communicate that information. It will help everyone, not just me and you, and that is a good thing for our organization. Unfortunately, your average lifespan at an organization is 16 months. What you leave in your wake after you leave is me, your teammate. I need that information to help you write acknowledgments, plan great events, and steward gifts effectively. If I don't know your donor's wife is allergic to something, I may mistakenly send her the wrong flowers because it's a nice thing to do.

Invite me to meetings from the beginning. I really need that seat at the table and that trust of you to bring me in the loop. I promise to be quiet and listen unless I have something really crucial to add. I'll never take credit for your idea or hard work, I just want to be there so I can help you from the start instead of being brought in too late at the end and creating a less than stellar product.

Don't assume I don't know what it's like to raise money. I do. I get it. Alumni and donor relations isn't a default for those who can't fundraise. I love my work and I want you to understand what drives me to help make fundraising successful at our organization. I actually have some great fundraising thoughts and want to help you.

Help me brainstorm on ways to help you engage and delight your donors. Please don't just drop an idea on me and walk away. Donors want three things: access, information, and experiences. They don't want coasters, tote bags, pens, honor rolls, and stuffy dinners. I can order a really thoughtful gift for your folks, but it won't have our logo on it. Allow me to be a creative professional and use the unique qualities of that donor to help surprise and delight them.

Do you see why it's important that you communicate that information to me?

Events don't fix anything. In fact, they're often drains on resources. They're not fundraising magic bullets to fix the fact that no one has visited these folks in a while. Events don't equal engagement. Let's work together to come up with another option for us to engage and recognize our donors. There's only so many heavy hors d'oeuvres a person can eat. Also, don't ever say the following words: *golf tournament*. Please and thank you, but NO.

Please, let's not promise anything to donors unless we know if it's possible. Let's review the gift agreement together and make sure we can deliver on the things the donor wants. Having to undo a promise is awkward and just no fun.

Finally, there are rules to fundraising.

They're there for a reason. AFP, CASE, IRS, etc etc. If I bring up these rules, don't fight me. I don't like them either. But they're there for a reason. They help protect you, me, and our donors. No one wants to feel smarmy. We want giving to be a joy, but it does involve paperwork. So help me get you and your donors through it. My goal in life is to never end up on the 11:00 news; I promised my mom. Help me keep my promise.

Regards,

Your friend in donor relations

PART 2

THE DONOR
RELATIONS
PROFESSION

MOM WAS RIGHT

DONOR RELATIONS AND DEVELOPMENT TRAINING AT ITS FINEST, FROM MOM!

As I sat on the train this morning, I was working on my next blog post while also wondering simultaneously if my mom would receive her Mother's Day card today. And then it hit me:

I am a donor relations professional because of my mother.

Put the non-applicable degrees aside and the years of experience, I learned Donor Relations and development fundamentals from a great source: Mom. I will go through the essentials and then you can comment and tell me if I am wrong...

1. The ability to write custom, personal hand-written thank you notes is a direct result of not being able to play with my birthday or Christmas presents until my notes were written. This is the core of what I do – giving gratitude – and my mom is an expert with note card and ink. She even made me practice extra in my big chief notebooks to make sure my script was legible and dignified, something that to this day I take great pride in. I have built many a relationship and strengthened others with a simple four sentence note of appreciation.

2. Ahh, how to have great table manners and etiquette, including her three big ones:

- Never order off of the kids menu

- Never be a difficult orderer (no sauce on the side here) – can we say hello to those people who RSVP to your events wanting a "South Beach Diet" entrée?

- Always deferring to the person "hosting you" to order the wine, and if we want to share appetizers, mimicking their ordering to make sure I was in line.

And this is why now, when I hire someone I always try to have at least one interview involving food!

3. The importance of *always* RSVPing – making sure that the hostess never had to follow up with me and we always made the deadline – how I wish everyone else felt this way!

4. Mother taught me the priceless etiquette of great gift-giving, making sure it is personal, custom, and purposeful, while still remembering her mantra: "Buy them something they wouldn't buy themselves." This eliminates the need for embarrassing dust collecting tchothckes in my work career and has allowed me to really wow some donors with great gifts!

5. There is the importance of relationship building, things like remembering names, knowing if someone is left handed for seating purposes, knowing favorite works of art and flowers, all of the little details that make people know you value their relationship. When a family would come over to visit, my mother would have a little something for each child (and to keep them occupied) and we *never* went to someone's home empty-handed.

6. Being the consummate hostess, my mother hosted many corporate parties, and that meant that she always attended to others' needs first and was the last one to

eat or drink at an event, a rule I still have for my team. I get to eat at the tastings, not at the events!

You too should be consumed with making sure everyone else's glasses and plates are full and never have anyone ask you where the trash can is because from across the room, you glide over and clear their plate or take away their empties. People notice this and love it!

7. You often need to fall on the "guest grenade" and have an inane in-depth conversation about whatever minutiae (like whether oaks or elms give better shade) is most important so that the most important person in the room can schmooze the way they need to. I've done this countless times in my career and the VP or President is always grateful.

8. When dealing with sticky situations, sometimes it's just better to beg forgiveness than ask permission. Do I need to explain?

9. There is no job too big or too small. I have seen her do everything from host a CEO and his family to cleaning cigarette butts out of her potted plants. This is essential for us to remember in donor relations.

10. Can you remember this one when you attend meetings about meetings? "If you don't have anything nice to say, don't say anything at all!"

11. Finally, the one I work on constantly... Patience, many things happen more slowly than we want them to, so we have to remember that sometimes, that's ok. And sometimes it may be a blessing, like I said- work in progress for those of you who know me personally...

Without these simple essentials that my mother taught me, I would not be the donor relations professional I am. I think of how blessed I was that all along, mom was right (of course) and was preparing me for a future. So be thankful if you learned these growing up as I did. And for those of you still learning them all, we all still have something to learn.

SWISS ARMY KNIVES & AMERICAN EXPRESS

BE PREPARED AND
MAKE YOURSELF STAND OUT

The last chapter was about Mom, so I better give a shout out to Dad. My dad, as many people know, is a great guy. He taught me many lessons growing up, one of which is to always be prepared. He never leaves his cabin at the top of the mountain without two things: a super duper Swiss Army knife and his American Express card. Now, he also brings his cell phone, but historically it has always been those two things.

So how does this relate to the donor relations profession? When I travel to speaking engagements and consultant jobs, I often hear the following

I work in donor relations, so I don't have a seat at the table.

No one treats me as a fundraising professional.

And now for the tough love. Is this something you perceive because it is true? And what have you done about it lately?

So, here we go with my philosophical list of tips and advice on this topic.

KNOW YOUR ROLE AND HOW YOU FIT INTO THE OVERALL FUNDRAISING PICTURE.

If you don't understand how important and essential donor relations is, then how are you going to communicate that to others? Can you define *donor relations* and *stewardship*? Do you know the key components of each and the difference between the two? If you don't, how do you expect anyone else to?

LOOK LIKE YOU BELONG

As my friend Paige says, "Don't bring your lunch into work in a Victoria's Secret bag and expect to be taken seriously." I love this because it sums up a great deal about donor relations as a profession, if we want a seat at the table, we *must* look and act like we belong.

BE INDISPENSABLE

Back to the Swiss Army knife and the AMEX. You must be indispensable. My dad and mom flew in to visit and Dad went to perform a simple fix in my apartment and because he couldn't take his trusty Swiss Army knife – thanks to the TSA – he was at a loss for his "go to" solution.

You *must* be your leadership's go to solution when in a pinch. My friends and I observe that some donor relations professionals are out of the office for vacation for 4 or more weeks and we chuckle at the idea of this! Can you imagine being so dispensable that you aren't needed for that long? Most of my VPs would have gone bonkers – and so would I – thinking of the important conversations, meetings, and work, we were missing!

BE A STRATEGIC THINKER

Donor relations is no longer the reactionary field it once was; now we must take the role of leading the organization's strategy with its constituents in partnership with leadership. If you don't have a strategic plan for donor relations at your organization, you are far behind the curve. Remember, we are all swimming in the same philanthropic ocean, and if I do it better, then the current streams my way.

Perform a stewardship audit, benchmark best practices and next practices, attend a conference, host a regional gathering of others in the field, hire a consultant to give you an outside perspective. The key here is *Do Something!* Your leadership will respect you and thank you for it; it shows initiative. It is no longer good enough to just keep to the status quo and keep your head down and not make waves.

SAY, "NO!"

It is perfectly acceptable for you to set boundaries with your program, as long as you have backup for your decisions. We as a profession and our personalities are mostly people pleasers and "yes" men and women.

It is time to stand up and be noticed that indeed, like a Swiss Army knife, you have specific functions, skills, and talent areas, and should be used for those. This would all be clear to your colleagues and leadership if you had that strategic plan. After all, have you ever used the toothpick from a Swiss Army knife to saw a branch? I thought not; the toothpick says, "No".

PRIORITIZE

You can't be everything to everyone, and if you have to make a decision as to who to say no to, ask your leadership to help you prioritize. This will garner you respect and save you from being labeled a Martyr in your organization, a label that, for a long time, donor relations has held proudly. Well, no longer. A savvy professional knows when to ask for help and leaders respect and admire that.

IT'S NOT ROCKET SCIENCE

EDUCATING OTHERS ON THE IMPORTANCE OF DONOR RELATIONS

As many of you know, it's really important to me to consistently move forward the profession of relationship building. In our world of donor relations, we are often seen as the bridge between the donor and the organization.

I can tell you that, lately, I've heard a great deal of feedback on the role of donor relations in an organization and that, combined with the data from the *Pulse of Donor Relations* survey tells us that the role is constantly shifting. It's changing for the better, but there still remains a large gap of understanding exactly what it is that makes up the donor relations profession.

Far too often, I hear fundraisers, peers, and others proclaim that not only does donor relations make complete sense for their organization, but that it's not "rocket science."

Sigh.

As I remain calm when people mention this to me, the following thoughts often run through my mind:

- Doing the right thing isn't rocket science, but so many seem to struggle with it as well.

- No one says this about making the ask, which, if prepped by proper donor relations, is no where near heart surgery either.

- It may not be rocket science, but only rocket science is, now isn't it?

- Have you ever seen donor relations gone wrong? Um, a little rocket science can't fix that.

- $!%#&^#$&*@#& – that's how I really feel.

- So no one has ever explained to you exactly what donor relations is, huh?

It is our duty, honor and privilege to educate others about our profession, but first we must know exactly where we're going and how to get there. It's our job not only to educate others, but also educate ourselves about the power and dynamism of donor relations. The impact that great donor relations can have on an organization is nothing short of powerful.

What have you done lately to help educate your teammates and peers? How do you answer the notion that donor relations is not "rocket science?" Is it a part of your onboarding process for new employees? Is donor relations a visible and central part of the development operation?

If you don't have answers to these questions, go out and get them.

The onus lies within us to educate others, to push our profession forward and to answer the call of a profession passionately. If you don't have passion for the work, there are other ways to spend your days. Me, I'm going to stay in the relationship business and serve as an advocate and ambassador. I hope you join me.

A SEAT AT THE TABLE

HOW TO EARN YOUR SEAT AT THE TABLE WITHOUT A HISSY FIT

Many donor relations professionals comment that they do not have a presence at important meetings, or don't feel that they have a seat at the table. I hear all the time, "She was well meaning and well-intentioned, but couldn't translate that to leadership."

How do we expect senior leadership to take us seriously when every email begins with, "I feel that..."? **It's important to be emotionally aware, but not emotional.** Passion can impede progress if not expressed in the right manner. It's time to take the emotion out of the situation and earn your seat at the table. Bring the value to them, show them the reasons why you should be present, other than, "Everyone else is sitting there, why not me?"

What kind of contributions can you make at a prospect management meeting or at a major gift strategy meeting? Sometimes your contribution is to be a good listener. My old boss used to call those "listening meetings", meaning I should be pleased I was at the table, but my primary function was to listen and absorb.

One great way to earn a seat at the table is to involve yourself in the onboarding and training process at your organization.

Do all new hires meet with you and/or your team within their first month? They should. It is important for you to be able to communicate the power and effectiveness of donor relations to the overall organizations to your teammates both new and old.

Also, are you providing them with resources for their professional development? You can provide them with links to the latest donor studies. You need to be the expert in the field, well informed and on top of the donor numbers, information, and strategy. Try to avoid being the place your teammates go to when they need an item, a choice of linen, or a blank notecard. These things are helpful, yes, and you can be the expert on those as well, but first they should know you are a professional in your field.

Another approach: what about building the table and inviting others to it? If you sit around in your office waiting for an email invite, you've got it all wrong! Get out there and have a conversation, prove the value of your seat, even if it's on the fringe at first, and then show them the impact of your presence. It's our responsibility to be proactive and strategic. You can't wait for an invite to the party; you need to have a party of your own!

We need to move beyond the idea that donor relations is a back office profession. We carry portfolios of donor visits, so we should be known across our organizations or campuses as a visible part of the fundraising team. If no one knows your face or name and you sit behind emails all day, you are setting yourself up for failure. Put on your extrovert hat and get out there!

THE FRONT LINE

GET OUT AND THANK SOMEBODY

When I first arrived on the fundraising landscape, there was a large divide between the "front office" and the "back office". Even though the divide still exists in some organizations both physically and philosophically, I am happy to say that donor relations is a key component of changing that paradigm.

Donor relations is no longer a reactive, stagnant position in many organizations. One of the things that has changed that is that donor relations professionals are leaving their offices – for more than events – more and more often. Many DR professionals now carry a portfolio of donors and are out on visits regularly. This benefits not just the development operation, but the donor as well.

Here is what I have seen and what I encourage my clients to do: Get out from behind the desk and thank somebody! Pair up with a front-line fundraiser and start taking donors out to say, "Thank you!" Then get out there on your own. Start first with local visits, thanking those who are closest, but who may not get seen by a gift officer regularly. Then the next time you go to a conference, go and visit donors there.

Now some of you are saying, won't my fundraisers be upset by me visiting "their" donors? Nope. Not if you talk to them first, start by pairing with them and have your leadership's backing. Everyone I have ever implemented this with was thankful to have another person to visit folks who might not get seen often.

Who are *those folks*? They are planned giving donors, donors in a multi-year pledge, mid-level donors, and others who may live more remotely. What can you do to help bridge the gap? Build trust and demonstrate that you're trying to help the overall organization and the donor who needs the attention. There are way more donors than there are fundraisers, so the numbers are on your side!

Remember these things:

- Take notes and fill out a wonderful contact report on the visit; this will help everyone.

- Follow up with a thank you note to the donor and an email to their primary prospect manager to let them know about the visit.

- Ask for more. You can do it and it will help you get a better pulse on your donors and their needs.

It's very difficult to build a donor relations program if you're not exposed to donors regularly.

ROUND, 3D, & ROBUST

THE DIFFERENCE BETWEEN
STEWARDSHIP & DONOR RELATIONS

Often, I am asked about my strong assertion that stewardship and donor relations are not synonymous. I believe that this clarification is crucial to the profession moving forward. We must be advocates of this difference and help explain it to others in order to build understanding and awareness.

The major difference is that stewardship is tied to the gift the donor gives; one cannot steward a donor, only their giving. But an organization can engage, cultivate, and relate to donors, with stewardship being one part of the overall donor relations strategy.

This is a vital distinction that cannot be overstated. Using the terms incorrectly blurs the clear divides of the work and can lead to confusion and error. If donor relations is proactive, then it must also be said that stewardship is reactive. Stewardship is the activity that takes place after the gift is received. Donor relations encompasses so much more, both in anticipation of the gift and in preparation for a long-term relationship that must be nurtured in order for positive philanthropy to occur.

In another metaphor, I look at stewardship as one or two dimensional, flat, and static. Donor relations should be sensory, round, three-dimensional, and robust. It is a dynamic part of the relationship that exists between donor and organization. If a shop of donor relations professionals is just cranking out stewardship reports and acknowledgments, this is the foundation and a good first step, but by no means is it all-encompassing, proactive donor relations. Far too often, when performing assessments of donor relations, I find that the professionals are task-oriented and busy, but that the work that results is much more gift-oriented than donor-oriented.

So how do we make the shift and also explain to others that while stewardship is a baseline, it isn't enough on its own? A donor *requires* stewardship but *desires* donor relations. Think of it as in education where you have prerequisites for classes. Stewardship is 101 and donor relations is 201. In order to advance a relationship, the prerequisite must be met.

THE DONOR RELATIONS MANTRA

WORDS TO GUIDE YOUR DECISION MAKING

Many times when I go to visit folks on their campuses, I learn a great deal about my own perspectives on donor relations than in my everyday work. I think sometimes we are so close to our own work, and we care so much, that we can often get lost in the forest of ideas. Often, it's a simple spark, a basic idea or mention of something that delighted a donor that sparks the greatest ideas.

As I interpret what choices to make as we innovate or take on new projects, I have a very simple mantra that guides all of my decision making. I hope you will adopt something similar in your areas. My donor relations mantra is this:

> *Does this benefit our donors? If it doesn't benefit a donor, we don't do it.*

You could cross apply this to alumni or constituents as you like.

This mantra could also help those of you who have difficulty saying "no" to new projects or ideas. I think for many of us, we have people who are always saying, "If you could just do this," or "Can't you add that?" which is not only frustrating because people aren't being respectful of the fact that you have other things to do, but it also is a fundamental breakdown in the idea that donor relations is not reactionary but is proactive and strategic.

I won't add anything to our plate unless it benefits the donors, *period*. At the end of the day, that's our purpose and mission, in careers and, for some of us, in life. At every turn, we must challenge assumptions that the activities we are performing are meaningful and strategic, the best return on investment and use of our time. The one simple line of, "If it doesn't benefit our donors, we don't do it," vastly simplifies this.

What is your donor relations mantra?

ENLIGHTENED DONOR RELATIONS

DO YOU HAVE IT?

Have you ever been somewhere with someone and thought, "This is exactly where I belong right now"? I know it sounds vague at first, but imagine if we gave that feeling to our donors time and time again.

The ultimate goal of enlightened philanthropy is to pair the donor's needs and desires to do good in the world with your organization's fundraising priorities. In order to do this in a heightened manner, two things are inextricable: the donor's desire and the organization's priorities. In THAT order. It doesn't work if you're constantly trying to shove your funding initiatives upon an uninterested party.

The same bodes true for donor relations. We need to match our donors' desires for gratitude, accountability, and recognition with our offerings. That's a donor focused program. It's difficult to make an individual fit into a system that wasn't built for them.

What I see a great deal is donor relations work that relies on process and policy and not necessarily to the highest philanthropic aim. Donors tell us time and time again they want three things: access, information, and experiences.

How do we provide them with the memorable? How do we demonstrate for them the impact of their philanthropy on our organizations? In some cases it can be easily accomplished; others allow us the opportunity to stretch our skills considerably.

The ultimate in donor relations and engagement usually surrounds having a donor meet the recipient of their generosity or see their money in action. This type of interaction tends to leave a lasting impression on both parties involved and directly connects donors to their dollars.

At a certain point of wealth, a person has enough coasters, public recognition, and plaques. But most philanthropists never stop learning, seeking new experiences, and ways to help others. It is our job and pleasure to connect them inextricably to their philanthropic priorities.

When I want to convey this message to leadership, I usually ask them to close their eyes and remember a time when they were really grateful at a certain time and place. Usually they can recall it vividly. Then translate that to your donors. What do we do to go above and beyond, to surprise and delight them? One of the key factors I look for in a great donor relations professional is that somewhat elusive "attitude of gratitude". I find that it is very difficult for someone who isn't grateful and thankful in their daily lives to be a wonderful fit in donor relations. You have to be a giver, full of gratitude and ways to share that with others.

Donors innately sense this. They know when the thank is sincere and when there is an ulterior motive. Gratitude is a lifestyle, and one I'm proud to carry with me wherever I go. How do we as donor relations professionals make this gratitude infectious? Transmitting this to others is just as important to our career as metrics and numbers, plans and strategy. What will you do today to have others understand that for many people that moment of sincere gratitude is like a moment of warm sunshine after a long winter.

$100,000 IN UNSOLICITED GIFTS

THE ROI OF DONOR RELATIONS

Having the opportunity to help organizations change their relationships with donors is a phenomenal privilege. Combine that with helping them realize a boost to their bottom line through donor relations and I'm in hog heaven!

Donor relations has a tangible return on investment, every time, in every way. And we can prove it. Throughout my travels, I meet people who say to me, "If only you knew the thrill of being a fundraiser." After I give them a major side eye, and note their nametag for future reference, I tell them that not only have I been a fundraiser, I *am* a fundraiser.

Donor relations makes money for an organization; more importantly, it keeps money from leaving. Here are some recent examples of ROI through donor relations.

One of my clients just redesigned their endowment reports and sent them out with a survey asking donors how they did. Not only did they receive wonderful feedback on their process and new reports, they also received over $25,000 in unsolicited gifts in those surveys.

Same thing for another client. They went through the same arduous process of revamping endowed fund stewardship, and while it was, at times, painful and frustrating, no one is mad at the over $75,000 they received unsolicited in the mail with their feedback surveys. That's $100,000 none of us would turn down if it showed up in our bank accounts.

Think about it in another way. If donor relations does their job well and becomes retention experts, then we can prove the ROI of retention on our first time donors and donors over time. My friends at the Agitator talk about donor retention all the time, and their facts are dead on.

So how do we prove the ROI of donor relations? We *must* track it. We need to look at retention rates, donors who upgrade, donors who make unsolicited gifts, and we need to say, "Wow! Look at all of the money coming in as a result of making the donation process a joyful one."

Acquisition of new donors is easy to track; it's also 7 times more expensive to obtain a new donor than it is to keep the one you have. What would a decrease of 10% in the acquisition budget and moving it to donor relations mean in terms of ROI? I can tell you , it means a great deal.

Why do these numbers matter? Because leadership needs and wants them. In order to advocate for more resources, donor relations has to show a tangible ROI of every effort we do, both large and small. When I quantify the impact of donor relations on an organization, heads begin to swivel, fundraisers begin to take notice, and the importance of donor relations rises. After all, it's very hard to ask for money from a donor who left your organization after their first donation.

HAVING FUN WHILE WORKING LIKE DOGS

SPENDING A LITTLE MORE TIME ENJOYING YOUR WORK

I absolutely love what I do! Fundraising and donor relations isn't just a job for me, it is my chosen career and, more than that, my vocation (autocorrect tried to make that *vacation*; irony).

I think it is absolutely essential that you love what you do for a living, not just collect a paycheck. If you're going to collect a paycheck, go to the for-profit world; at least your paycheck will be bigger! That all being said, at times I find myself in my travels and at conferences thinking, "Boy, do these folks take themselves a tad bit seriously." It's true our jobs come with risk and reward; anytime you deal with money, sensitive legal and ethical issues abound. But in all honesty, one of the great joys of my life is being able to say that if I send one too many thank you notes to someone, they don't die. It helps now that I've stopped mailing things to dead people.

As previous stated, I do take offense when someone says, "It's donor relations, not rocket science," and I quietly point out that while the concept is simple, the execution is not. Well, that and then I tell them I can do differential equations in my head and ask them to do one with me...I digress.

It sounds overly simplistic and quite contrite, but it's true. I don't have the stomach or nerves to be in the brain surgery business. I'm happy and passionate about supporting those folks though. What I want most for us is to enjoy ourselves in our work, especially during the stressful times like fiscal year-end. I don't want you to think that I don't take my work seriously. I do, nothing causes me more pain than a crooked label, but at the same time do it with good humor.

For those of you who have heard me speak, you know I love a witty joke, especially if it is ill-timed and sometimes inappropriate! But in all truth, I make my audiences laugh because far too often I see them leave sessions looking like they ate something bad inside. I want them to leave mine feeling laughter and energy. Most people appreciate it, some don't, like the attendee who once wrote that, "I'm not here to be entertained, I'm here to be informed." Yup, I still remember it word-for-word. It hurt for a long time and now I use it as a powerful motivation to do both.

Why can we not do the same with our donors and our constituents? We can. Let's spend a little more time laughing and enjoying the work that we do. Not all of them are stiff and no fun; in fact most of them are a blast! They're human remember?

My former VP, Dawn, always fondly recalls her favorite stint at a job, saying, "We worked like dogs all day and all night, but boy did we have fun and laugh a lot." That's the kind of job I look for and want.

SHOULD I STAY OR SHOULD I GO?

WHEN IS LOYALTY TOO LONG?

The career path of either a fundraising or donor relations professional is an interesting one. After many conversations, it becomes even clearer to me that many of us view our profession in quite contrasting lights.

I can honestly say that I have never met anyone in the industry who grew up dreaming of being a non-profit fundraiser or relationship professional. None of us majored in it in college. But here we are. And where are we going? I had the pleasure of meeting a young lady on a client visit; she was an undergraduate and was also our server at dinner. She planned on a career in non-profit work by majoring in marketing and minoring in social work. Smart cookie.

Many of us never thought of our career trajectory when we got into this field, and now we find ourselves faced with interesting realities. Like any profession, ours has devolved into a serious career choice for folks and many are now majoring in philanthropy in college. But what does our career path look like?

As I quoted before, the fact is in the United States, the average lifespan of a fundraiser currently stands at 16 months. You can see that fact in the *Chronicle of Philanthropy*. So that's the average, meaning some stay much shorter and some much longer. So how do we know when is the right time to stay or go? It's no good to be seen as a job hopper (the "Haaaper" commercial pops into my head), but can you also hurt your career by sticking in one position too long? The answer is a resounding YES.

The donor relations world has seen some interesting position shifts in the past 18 months with those at the top leaving jobs for others, being phased out, or moving upward significantly. This begs the question, when is loyalty too long? It's a fact in our business that in order to be compensated well, you have to leave or seriously threaten it. But what are other reasons to leave? Certainly new challenges and different types of organizations are a good reason. Stagnancy in leadership being another, but so is a change in leadership. There is a growing sense of impatience in the business with the demand for doing more with less, wanting the new shiny thing from our leadership.

So what's the solution? Pick it up and pack it up in order to advance. Yup, most often that's the reality. So how do we retain top talent? How do you build loyalty and long tenures without accepting complacency. How do you stay somewhere more than 5 years and not be seen as the "dinosaur" in the office? How do you keep talent and not let it get poached? In certain markets like Boston, DC, and New York, the revolving doors spin wildly as organizations poach talent in a competitive race for dollars and donors.

Speaking of donors, what is best for them and our organizations? How does one balance their need for personal success and fulfillment with that of a mission you believe in? These are issues we should be discussing at conferences, in blogs, and at gatherings. We should work to advance our profession and realize that it's just that, a profession and a vocation. How do we beat the drum for change without losing sight of the overall goal of inspired philanthropy? Who helps us mold our career trajectories and paths to success if it's not us?

STUCK IN THE MUD

STOP BEING REACTIONARY AND MOVE FORWARD

One of the biggest differences in the past few years in the evolution of donor relations and stewardship as a profession – and area of intense focus for most fundraising shops – is the progression of thought about donors and our activities surrounding them. Yes, we are becoming more donor-focused than ever, with most of us taking the mantra, "If it benefits our donor and our relationship with them, we must do it."

Many people constantly ask me what the new face of donor relations will look like, and the answer for me is basic: strategic, forward-thinking donor relations programs are not only the future, they are the here and now.

When the profession began, it began out of necessity. Who was going to provide things and services for donors that fundraisers didn't have the time or resources to do? Let's give it to donor relations; they are the reactors. Problem solvers. Those who get it done.

The problem with this type of mindset toward donor relations is that it is reactive, transactional, and does not allow for planning and forward-thinking. If you're always reacting and doing the tasks, how do you plan for the future?

Now, donor relations and stewardship, at least those who run sophisticated, donor-focused strategic shops, is largely proactive, relationship-based, and forward-looking. So, how do you change a reactionary, task-oriented program into a strategic innovative one and what does that look like? Here are some tips.

ANTICIPATE THE NEEDS OF YOUR DONORS

Stop waiting for gifts and situations to happen to your organization and anticipate the needs of your donors before requests happen. The best way to do this? Obtain feedback from your current constituency about their needs and desires for the future.

CREATE STRATEGIC PLANS AROUND EACH AREA OF YOUR OPERATIONS

Let me be clear, these aren't lists of tasks you do as a result of a gift; these are initiatives that fall into place when giving happens. Do you have this for acknowledgments, reporting, naming opportunities, events, and do you have a program that fills the gaps? How are you working with your data team to find rich data streams that will allow robust analysis of your constituency? Remember, data always drives your strategy; be it from your database, peers, donors, or other places, your strategy must have solid roots.

FIND PATHWAYS TO DIRECT CONTACT WITH YOUR DONORS

Your contact with them should be holistic in manner and not just when they call to RSVP or need parking or catering advice. You should have a portfolio of relationships that you help maintain and service, always looking for the forward thinking opportunity to build from.

CONSIDER A BLANKET STEWARDSHIP PROGRAM

Have you thought lately about those donors that fall through the cracks? What are you doing for them? Consider a blanket stewardship program that can cover multiple populations through the implementation of a measured, strategic combination of communications, unique opportunities, and other items, engaging your donors across multiple platforms and experiences.

EVALUATE YOUR PROGRAM

Have you evaluated your program from a metrics and ROI based approach lately? How cost effective are your efforts? Are they working for your populations? I'm not talking a task audit here folks, I'm talking about real dissection of your programs, evaluating efficiencies, ways in which you are involved across your department, and whether or not everything you do is donor-focused or if you are just doing it because you always have.

CARVE OUT TIME

Finally, in order to be strategic and forward-thinking, dare I say groundbreaking and innovative, you need to have the time to do so.

If you are constantly fighting to keep up, how can you make forward progress?

CHECKERS vs CHESS

GET STRATEGIC AND PROACTIVE

As donor relations evolves as a profession, one of the questions I field most often is how to transform a reactive donor relations shop into a proactive donor relations shop. And therein lies the great divide. Just like education allows people to have more choice and option in their life, being a proactive donor relations professional allows so many more choices than being reactive, which only allows for one path.

If you always have your head down producing results as you have done them in the past, you have no options to look ahead to the future and become strategic about your work. If you're always doing the same work over and over, how can you be innovative? It requires huge discipline and planning to truly become proactive and strategic, but there is no better time than now to start.

For me, it begins with an assessment of the program, a good, cold, hard look at where the donor relations shop spends its time and how donors benefit from time used. Are there particular processes that are laborious and tedious? Is there waste happening? Have you surveyed or obtained feedback from you donors to ensure you are building a program they will appreciate and desire or are you operating off of assumptions?

You see, it's a lot like checkers and chess. Checkers is a short-term limited game with predictable outcomes. This would be your reactive donor relations shop. Chess is a strategic long game, with unpredictable twists and turns that can have long-term results and a vision that is multiple steps ahead. The two are not interchangeable. Our donors deserve chess champions.

The second step after assessing your current program is to obtain feedback from your donors on your current activities and evaluate what is successful and what is losing the game.

After that, it's time to look to other programs you admire or those that are proactive and strategic to find out what they do in order to become successful. It boils down to choice, they will tell you. Like in checkers, if you only have one type of playing piece, you are limited. In chess, you have a wide variety, which gives you great choice. Deft moves can be made and game plans switched throughout the game of chess that opens up new paths to victory. Can you say this about your donor relations program? If you can't, now is the time for change.

After you find new ideas and a new direction for your game plan, it's time to bring it to your leadership to gain their buy-in and support. This step is crucial. Once you have their buy in, your field of play opens greatly to the possibilities of strategy. Then it's all about the implementation from there.

Check. Mate.

GPS COORDINATES OF MY WELL

RECOGNITION, STEWARDSHIP, AND TRUST

I am fortunate that, as part of my travels, I have had the wonderful opportunity to listen to many wonderful speakers. One of the speakers I had the good fortune to hear was explaining the relationship between major donors and organizations. Among his many salient points was the following nugget that I quickly added into my iPad to discuss with you. "Recognition is not motivational, stewardship is. Trust is experiential." Profound in its simplicity, eh? But it really strikes at the core of not only what we do as fundraising professionals, but also why we do it.

Let's boil it down into its parts and then look at the whole in terms of the relationships we ask people to have with our organizations.

RECOGNITION IS NOT MOTIVATIONAL

This strikes close to home, especially when you examine the amount of time fundraisers spend on public recognition of gifts, falsely believing that entrance into the platinum giving society over the titanium one will motivate a donor to stroke an extra-big check this time. It also relates back to my feelings on donor honor rolls. Very, *very* seldom do these types of recognition motivate donors to give, yet we seem to spend a great deal of time in their service.

STEWARDSHIP IS MOTIVATIONAL

Amen! If you, as a non-profit, spend my money according to the purpose it was given, tell me how you spent the money, and then tell me the impact it had on others, I'll give to you forever. Stewardship builds loyalty, it reinforces good behavior and builds trust in the organization.

As many of you know, I think Charity:Water is the best in the business at this. They not only tell me how they spend my money, they send me the GPS coordinates of the well my funds helped drill! They do this regardless of the amount of my gift. How come other non-profits, universities included, fail so spectacularly at this? We ask, nearly beg, for unrestricted funding, yet these are the folks we communicate with about the impact of their giving the least. How does this make sense? If there is truly an area of greatest need, then for the love of all that is holy, tell me what that need was and how my money made a difference! It doesn't have to be glamorous; tell me I paid the light bill, bought reams of copy paper, anything, but tell me something!

TRUST IS EXPERIENTIAL

If you've ever been burned by giving your trust too freely, you can literally still feel the sting of betrayal. It's a palpable feeling that never does seem to recede all the way. When an organization breaks a donor's trust, the road is long and hard and full of painful rocks. Many years of good relationship building is lost in one simple breech of trust, and safe to say in many cases, people aren't forgiving, nor should they be. You solicit a donor for money and then don't spend it because your department chair is saving for the day Bruce Willis arrives on a spaceship? Well that's a tough second ask, now isn't it? There's forgiving, and then there's blind trust. Your organization must be trustworthy in order to have donors invest in it and maintain their giving.

SAL THE EVIL SHREDDER

ARE YOUR DONOR
COMMUNICATIONS EFFECTIVE?

In a recent presentation, the presenter cited research (2012) that said only 7% of your donors read the communications you send thoroughly. Seven. I was not surprised that the number was low, but I was a bit miffed at exactly how low. Though sometimes when I open my mail and email, I know why it's so low. If this were a measure of success, we would receive an F-.

Are we giving our donors things they want to read, things that draw them in and make it worth their time? Have we asked them what they want to read and in what format they want to read it in? If not, are we just throwing messaging into a dark abyss and hoping they catch it and read it?

Old wisdom of direct mail and publications says time and time again that the longer the appeal letter, the more people give. There are even whole books on this topic. Most of this science comes from the non-profit world, not higher-ed or healthcare.

Would this still hold true now? For your audience? I would beg to argue that point. In an information overloaded society, if you send me a 4-page solicitation letter, personally, there's no chance I'm reading it. But if you send me a postcard with a telling image and a concise message, I'll take action.

What do you think?

I think that the times have changed greatly and we haven't changed with them. How have you changed your communications to adapt to the changing landscape of readership? Do you know what your donors are reading? Have you asked them? Why not?

One effective thing to do is to ask your donors their preferred communication channel (mail, phone, email, social media) and speak to them through that channel primarily. Not eliminating the others, but being intentional about how you group your donors, other than giving amount. Or bucket them all based on age, assuming that most, if not all, 35 or 85 year olds behave the same, a shallow assumption indeed.

There's a shredder beneath our mailboxes in my apartment building for a reason. As I came back from a recent trip, my held mail contained 12 pieces from charitable organizations; all but one were in letter format and also were thick. (Insert your favorite shredding noise here.) One was a well-done graphic postcard that had an image of students holding up the letters "THANK YOU" and a great short message. Thanks, UMass Boston, your next gift is coming soon because your postcard is on my fridge.

For those non-profits who sent me lengthy letters and "gifts" like address labels, yours met an evil shredder named Sal (What, you don't have a name for your shredder?) He's a hungry little thing. When he struggles to shred your mailing and groans in protest, I think we have a problem (and I sincerely hope you didn't send me a nickel, Sal hates Nickels, spits them back at my head). Nothing like a flying nickel or saint token coming back at you from Sal the shredder to wake you up!

So how do we effect change? How do we prove to those experts that the old format of lengthy letters and "gifts" is a ruse and we see right through it. Ask them the last time they have verifiable data with YOUR population, ask your folks. Also, every time a communication comes to you for review, ask yourself if you would turn it over or open it and read it. Who's your audience? Is this putting your best foot forward? If not, begin a discussion about change.

THE BIG BLINKING NEON SIGN

WHY HONOR ROLLS OF DONORS ARE THE MOST WASTEFUL DONOR RELATIONS PRACTICE POSSIBLE

There are many things I believe we do in donor relations that make absolutely no sense. Top of my list is the honor roll of donors. I hope you read this post and share it with as many others in the non-profit world as humanly possible.

In all my time in donor relations, I have never heard of a donor who gave an organization a million-dollar gift because their name was in a textual list of donors. Yet I must get asked at least once a week what I think of honor rolls and their place in donor recognition and stewardship. I think they have no useful purpose, they provide opportunities to make costly mistakes, they are a huge waste of human resources, time, money, and they are otherwise foolish.

Why honor rolls don't provide any benefit

Time and time again, we have asked donors what they want and how they want to be recognized, and the three things that appear most often in their answers are: access, information, experiences.

Donors want handwritten notes from students. They want to meet those that benefit from their philanthropy. They don't care about your honor roll, only you do. Just because you have always done them does not make honor rolls a great idea.

A list, a list of names, does not tell a story. If an image is worth a thousand words, a donor honor roll is silence.

HONOR ROLLS ACTUALLY HURT DONOR RELATIONS

In major cities, honor rolls are passed around from research office to research office, basically telling your competitors where to find the money. Talk about a privacy violation! From the donors' perspective, you might as well put a big blinking neon sign above each of their heads that says, "I give money away!"

WHAT YOU SHOULD DO INSTEAD

If we took the time and effort that goes into producing monstrously ineffective honor rolls, and pooled those resources instead into a piece on the impact of a gift, the story behind the gift, and the story behind the donor, then we would be much more effective in recognizing the people behind the gift. Those people and their stories are what truly makes philanthropy possible.

I have yet to hear a person who works at an organization that produces an honor roll say, "It's so easy, I just push a button and voila!" or "I've never heard a complaint."

So I ask you in the clearest, most relevant way I can to stop it. Stop doing them. Eliminate all honor rolls, all the time.

I've helped to eliminate honor rolls at many institutions. Every single time, we have saved money, staff time, and other countless hours of grief. Every time, the honor rolls went away without a complaint. In their place, we have been able to build robust and meaningful donor relations programs, with tangible ROI and with storytelling that is meaningful to donors.

OCCUPATIONAL HAZARDS

DO PEOPLE KNOW WHAT YOU DO?

BY DEBBIE MEYERS

By nature, DR practitioners tend to have behind-the-scenes personalities. We don't share the limelight; we create it. We are other-focused, making sure donors feel good, not worrying about ourselves. And that's fine, because that's what we're paid to do. But beware of these cold hard truths:

1. If people don't know what you do, they assume you do nothing.

2. Perception is everything.

Our colleagues may see us handle donor correspondence, create name tags and arrange meetings for donors, and view us administrative assistants. If they see us managing events, they may assume can cater. Or worse yet, they never see what we do, or, if they do see what we do, they fail to attribute it to our efforts.

When you think about it, anything relating to donors is considered donor relations. So where do you – or more importantly, where does your boss – draw the line? If ever a career existed that's a magnet for the catch-all "other duties as assigned" bullet in its job description, it's ours.

Moreover, because our work says "Thank you" instead of "please" – i.e., we step in after a gift has come in – we can be viewed as a cost center rather than a revenue-producing area. We spend money. Of course, what we spend often generates more and bigger gifts from well stewarded donors, but that's not always obvious to higher-ups. Some institutions view our profession as a luxury and not a necessity.

In fact, I once left a job because the institution's new leader wasn't invested in recognition events. After he asked the question that proved his mindset – "Wouldn't our time be better spent asking for new gifts instead of thanking people who already gave?" – I immediately updated my resume.

It's bad enough being seen as neutral. It's even worse when you're thought of as a negative, a part of the organization that spends money, can be easily replaced and is subservient.

That's why it's crucial that we promote ourselves and our work. We cannot afford to passively go through our professional lives and shrug our shoulders, saying, "Oh, well, if that's what they think of me, that's their problem." To protect our profession, our livelihood and our self esteem, we have to prove our worth. Every day is an opportunity to answer your employer's question, "What have you done for me lately?"

You can do that in two ways: metrics and PR.

Metrics are a sticky wicket. Two key concepts:

MEASURE WHAT YOU VALUE, AND VALUE WHAT YOU MEASURE

Identify metrics that are meaningful to your organization. Is it renewed memberships? Increased gifts? Donor retention? Event participation that led to more gifts? Ask your Powers-

That-Be what they value. And ask your donors. Use surveys, focus groups, informal phone calls – whatever works.

KNOW THE DIFFERENCE BETWEEN CORRELATION AND CAUSATION

We rarely will be able to know that something we did caused a donor to make a gift, but we frequently can assert that what we did is related to that giving. If you report on an endowed fund, and two months later, the donor makes a gift to that fund, you can confidently say those two actions (reporting – giving) are related.

As for PR, there are two key concepts.

EDUCATE THE MASSES

By disseminating information that is useful to others, you naturally will position yourself as a resource and an expert. Offer to lead educational sessions. Email articles, forward checklists, provide summary memos of your results after a big project. Make house calls: informal, like a drop-by just to see how a gift officer is doing; and formal, like a scheduled, focused presentation among your customers.

YOU DON'T HAVE TO BRAG ABOUT YOURSELF TO MAKE PEOPLE AWARE OF THE GOOD THAT YOU DO

Channel your inner Walter Brennan: "No brag, just fact." Don't be shy. You can't do your job if you don't let people know what your job is. Once you've gathered your metrics, let your colleagues know in objective, measurable terms how you can help them. The more you prove your value, the more likely you will be to find yourself at the table where decisions are made.

At conferences, I have heard examples of how DR professionals use metrics as well as clever, creative ways that they let their customers, higher-ups, and colleagues know what they have to offer. Please list yours below if you're willing to share.

This is our profession, and your career. Make the time to measure and share how valuable you are. And you are. That's a fact.

SPIKE LEE AND DONOR RELATIONS

ALWAYS DO THE RIGHT THING

So I'm not here to talk about the Knicks, but I am here to tell you about the challenges that we face in the sensitive area of donor relations. Anytime there are large amounts of money involved, and anytime there is a great deal at stake, murky waters arrive.

So here is the advice I'm going to give you that I borrowed from my friend Spike: DO THE RIGHT THING. Every time, every day, in every way.

Fight the good fight and always be on the right side of the rules when it comes to donor relations. Here's why; it may not always be easy, it may not always win you friends on your staff, but at the end of the day, you can look yourself in the mirror and not worry about ending up on the 11:00 news. Or even worse, on the front page of the *Chronicle of Philanthropy* or *New York Times*.

It isn't always easy to do the right thing when it comes to donations and donors; there is a great deal of pressure. And in fact, in our industry, everyone doesn't always send the right message. As a consultant, when I get on my soapbox, I often hear people say that "Organization X across the street does it that way so it must be okay" or "It's such a small thing, who will care?" I care, and you should, too.

Here are some of the sticky things we face that I want you to know about and avoid any entanglements at all.

- Quid Pro Quo laws and token gift items

- Allowing donors to pay pledges or buy event tickets with Donor Advised Fund monies

- Fudging matching gift forms to ensure the match goes through

- FERPA violations of sharing student data without their permission

- Allowing donors to be involved – at ALL – in the selection of their scholarship or faculty chair recipients

- Not spending donor monies the way you agreed to

- Having donor relations involved in how the money is spent (ie. donor relations awarding scholarships)

- Not protecting your donor's sensitive data

- Over promising deliverables in gift agreements that you can't deliver

- Not counting or booking gifts correctly to enhance numbers or giving percentages

Now, I'm not Chicken Little and the sky isn't falling. But I can tell you every time I read a headline that involves this, I just shake my head and I hope it's not someone I know. You need to be aware, and you need to make your leadership aware. Keep running the flag up the pole until someone listens and takes action.

You will never regret doing the right thing.

5 HANDWRITTEN NOTES

AND OTHER WAYS BOARD MEMBERS CAN DO DONOR RELATIONS

I often hear from peers just how difficult it is to engage volunteers, specifically board members in the fundraising process. As with many things, I look to donor relations for the solution.

Many of us have development committees of the board, but how many of us have donor relations committees? More of us should not just have a committee dedicated to the thank, but an entire board who "gets it." Leading up is part of the art and science of donor relations, so why not start at the very top!?

But how? I have a few tangible ideas for you to implement with your board. Not only are these ideas effective, but they will also start to create a new bridge to the idea that philanthropy is about so much more than the ask. Of all of the fundraising activities that we do, the ask is actually less than one percent of our time. So why do so many folks spend all their time focusing on it? Why is it that when we go to conferences, there are 10 or more sessions on solicitations, but less than three on thanking donors and cultivating relationships? Here's your turn to help shape that paradigm.

- Take a portion of the next board meeting and have an "attitude of gratitude" session. Teach your board why the simple act of saying thank you is so valued among your donors.

- Start having them each write five handwritten notes at each board meeting. Start by having them thank loyal donors.

- Have a thank-a-thon phone calling session at the next retreat where they call donors, you pick the segments, to say thank you. These calls are powerful for both people involved.

- Teach them about all the other activities they can participate in outside of solicitation. Where do you need help most?

- Bring a student or beneficiary into the board meeting to have them tell their story of how the support has changed their lives.

- Take a portion of the board meeting and have them tell why they give back. Record this information so you can help them be reminded of why they are key to your organization. These stories are invaluable to you.

- Understand that these are super-busy folks, so communicate with them in bullets or top points. I do an email called top five Friday that lists five unique but quick things they can do to help move a relationship forward. Each item should take less than 5 minutes.

How do you help your board live the donor relations centered life?

OUTSOURCING DONOR RELATIONS?

WAYS TO LIGHTEN YOUR WORKLOAD

I thought that headline might draw you in.

Often, when I am at conferences or consulting for folks, I hear a common thread, "I just don't have time for those innovative, new ideas." When I dig deeper and find out why, many donor relations folks are mired with tasks and the act of doing, rather than being able to lift their heads up and strategize for the future.

I have shared this common problem since I started my work in donor relations as a one woman shop, now on a team of six (which sometimes is *more* work) and have found that the solution often lies in two sources: technology and letting it go (cue that *Frozen* song that now is stuck in your head; you're welcome).

If you're techno-friendly, then that isn't an issue, but what about that whole letting it go idea? Donor relations folks, by their nature, are a wee bit controlling (Ahem, understatement of the century.) So how do we begin to let go and make strategic decisions about outsourcing some of our work, not just to vendors, but to others on our team? So here's the plan for you.

WHAT IS THE COST?

For every task and item that you do, you need to figure out how much it costs, not just fiscally, but in human hours and time. How much is it costing you hourly? Calculate your hourly rate, the one you're supposed to work, not actual hours. I did that once and figured out it was around $3 an hour. But my real rate based on my 37.5 hour work week is something we calculate into all of our efforts. Where is my time best spent? What are the things I'm really good at (some of you will say everything of course because we're perfectionists, too), but how long did it take you to get it perfect?

For example: I'm a pretty good wiz technologically, and have mastered most of Excel, however, if I want to make my data rich spreadsheet print pretty and look divine, I could spend hours. Instead, I give that to a staff member who in 10 minutes or so has me looking brilliant and completely competent to leadership by producing the best looking, easily readable spreadsheets you have ever seen. Boy, do I have them fooled. It's about identifying talents and optimizing time.

UNDERSTAND THE THINGS YOU CANNOT AND WILL NOT EVER OUTSOURCE

A couple of examples: endowment reports, recognition events, acknowledgments, and other things that need a careful eye and a good steward. Last year I heard of a prestigious liberal arts college that was outsourcing all of their endowment reports to a printer, sending them bulk rate mail and never proofing or seeing them before they went in the mail. The thought of it now sends chills up my spine. True, they were saving money and it was efficient to send data out and never see it again, but imagine if there were one mistake, in addition, endowment donors deserve better than that.

FIND AMAZING PARTNERS

I'm not just talking about vendors here, folks. Recently, I was on a campus and heard about how they wanted to digitally catalogue all of their named spaces and plaques for posterity.

Brilliant plan, one I did at Rollins that won a CASE award. But you know what? I didn't go photograph and document them all; I hired student interns to do the project. My student interns, although fiscally unpaid, were paid in leftover food, experience, and reference letters. They, in turn, were able to help with invaluable projects that would require me to be out of the office too much or were too overwhelming to accomplish.

The same goes for vendors. Some of the best relationships I have built with them were when I relied on their skills and expertise to help me out. Here are a few examples: postcard mailings, variable data projects, design work for print pieces, campaign launch events, thank-a-thons, and other creative efforts.

MAKE OTHERS TAKE RESPONSIBILITY FOR THEIR OWN WORK

Donor relations folks are the ones that can never seem to set boundaries and say, "No." That's why we end up ordering tchotchkes for alumni relations, catering for staff retreats, writing hand-written notes for development officers that are calligraphically-challenged, and sheriff badges for AVPs (that's another story).

Instead, we should spend our time building strategy and plans for implementation, then teaching other departments how to fish. An example: build together with your annual giving department a plan for annual giving stewardship, put all of the pieces in place, and let them execute the plan. You are involved and supportive, but not overburdened by the tasks. Instead you can build strategies that are donor-centric and responsible uses of your time.

I hope I have given you some tips and techniques for outsourcing some of your daily burdens. It's about how we can work smarter and be more strategic, not showing everyone how busy we are with tasks. Leadership respects vision and strategy, not long lists of todos.

LONGING FOR SMALL SHOP DAYS

ADVANTAGES OF SMALL ORGANIZATIONS

As many of you return from conferences – brains overloaded and chock full of new ideas, enthusiasm renewed by the energy of others – I hope you'll take this time to listen to me contemplate what I miss most about the small/solo shop days of donor relations for me. I hope some of you can relate.

When I first started in donor relations, it was me against the world (some of you know exactly what I'm talking about). Others of you haven't experienced donor relations without a staff, but can learn a great deal from those solo warriors. I longingly look back on those days with a sense of nostalgia and look for clues and hints that I can apply to my work as a leader of a team and a member of a development staff of over 100. Here are some of my thoughts.

BEING NIMBLE

Being a small or one-person shop makes you nimble and agile. You have more freedom to implement new ideas and react quickly, meeting changing donor needs without reinventing the wheel and causing a systematic and bureaucratic shift.

LACKING RESOURCES MAKES YOU MORE CREATIVE

When I had zero budget, no advocates, and no seat at the table, I believe that necessity was the mother of all invention, hence my love affair with technology. I was always looking for better, faster, and cheaper, simply out of necessity and the drive to change my workload.

MANAGING PEOPLE IS HARD WORK

I was recently helping on another campus down south (thanks for the grits!) and someone asked me, "What's the hardest thing I do?" It's to manage people. If done well, it takes a great deal of time and effort, and sometimes I find it draining and wish there was an easier way. The fact remains that there isn't an easier way. I miss the days when I had to mange myself and navigate political waters; the higher up you go, the more directions you mange in. I thrill and excite from the doing and the helping, the strategy and the execution. At times the management waters make me feel like I'm only treading until the next wave. And, Lord, help the person who has to manage me.

TIME MANAGEMENT

When I was a one-person shop, I was much more effective with my time. It was calendared, organized, and transparent, meetings with my department...uhm, myself...were quick and effective. I often lost arguments with myself, but that's another story for another day. Now, I often am torn between attending a meeting (and believe me, I'm happy to be invited) that becomes a time suck and implementing my strategies. It's a tough balance and something we don't spend enough time on professional development-wise, but it is crucial to our success.

BIGGER ISN'T ALWAYS BETTER

Take giving societies for example, just because you have 20 of them, doesn't mean they have meaning or benefit to your donors, simplifying is often the right direction. I have

4 and some days that's all a staff of 6 can do to keep them afloat successfully. Also, your staff and leadership is more accessible. Take advantage, seek out their opinions and time. For those of you on large campuses, now is the time to get out there and make sure people know who you are and what you do, which is hard when there are 200 development officers, but it can be done!

This returns back to my old conference motto:

> *Instead of implementing all of your takeaways now, improve one thing, do it well, turn it into great, and then move on to the next.*

Easy victories are still victories, I'll take a quick win over the status quo every day of the year. Find what you can improve and get to work, saving the large battles and epic Homerian wars for later, otherwise you get bogged down.

And finally, for those of you who are, like me, blessed to have staff, take time to appreciate it (even when everyone calls in sick). Also, reach out to share and lend a hand to those who don't have writers, editors, events people, coordinators, and assistant directors. Share your resources and help teach them the way. Someone did that for me when I first started and I'm still grateful for the development community that is so willing to help.

R-E-L-A-T-I-O-N-S

LESSONS LEARNED IN DONOR RELATIONS

BY DEBBIE MEYERS

We love lists. Top three ways, top five mistakes, Letterman's top ten. Bulleted and numbered lists, particularly with pictures, help us condense complex ideas or remember lengthy instructions. And mnemonics: "every good boy does fine" for treble clef, "roy-g-biv" for colors of the spectrum.

So here's my top-ten list of lessons learned in my donor relations career, with a helpful mnemonic (RELATIONS!)

R IS FOR READ

Author Stephen King says, "If you want to be a writer, you must do two things above all others: read a lot and write a lot." Ever wonder why you had to write all those pesky papers in school? And why they were so hard to write? Because you weren't sure what to say. It's not that you didn't know what the underlying themes were in a novel; the problem was there were so many!

Writing forces you to choose what to include and exclude. It makes you come to the point. If you're a good writer, you've got a great shot at being a clear thinker and an articulate speaker – all great skills for donor relations. So read!

E IS FOR EXPECTATIONS

Know what is expected of you. Every chance you get, prove you're doing it.

Recently, I heard about an annual giving director who worked like crazy to get her school's participation rate up, only to find out that her boss was more interested in actual dollars. Do you know what your boss expects of you? Or are you doing what *you* think you should be doing, or working on only the things *you* like and are good at?

Sounds simple, but have a clear plan in place for yourself or your department, articulate that plan to your supervisor and peers, and ask them for a constant evaluation on how you are doing. At worst, they'll say you need to improve. At best, they'll praise you for a job well done.

L IS FOR LISTEN

In life and on the job, practice active listening skills: your eyes open and attentive, mouth closed, body language relaxed and open.

With irate donors, let them do the talking. Refrain from defending yourself and take the time and patience to hear what they are truly upset about. Ask yourself why the person is upset. When you have that answer, ask why again. Keep asking why until you get to the real issue.

Then you can do your job effectively and heal that relationship.

One time, I tried to explain to a donor why he got a pledge reminder when he had already paid the pledge for his fellowship. I got into this detailed story about how data is pulled and then it has to be reviewed and obviously our paths crossed in the mail... He shut me up quickly by saying, "I don't care how you do it. Just fix it."

He then went on to talk about how important the fellowship was to him, and why he established it. This wasn't about a computer or data glitch that made him cranky. It was about something he valued deeply, and the trust he wanted to have in our ability to steward his fund well. You can't fix the past, but by listening carefully, you can learn how to repair the present and prepare for the future.

A IS FOR ASSERTIVE

Our profession often dictates that we remain in the background so the spotlight is on our donors and our organization. Sometimes it requires us to fall on the sword for someone else in our organization, for the good of the cause. And that's fine. But it doesn't mean we have to be martyrs or doormats.

As donor relations practitioners, we constantly battle the perception that our main contributions are tying bows and throwing parties. The difference between planning a party and planning an effective donor appreciation event is like the difference between affixing a band aid and curing a disease. A strategically planned event with meaningful messaging and clearly articulated outcomes can change a donor's life and your institution's future. A well written endowment report that shows impact and gratitude can lead to a multi-million dollar gift.

So if you want a seat at the decision-making table, ask for it. If you want a promotion and can show objective value to your organization, ask for it. If you need more staff to make a bigger impact on your institution's ability to nurture donors and raise more money, ask for it. Hmmm, maybe A is for ASK!

T IS FOR TEAM

Play well with others on your team. Get to know your team. Learn who can help you reach success, and determine how you fit in with the rest of the team.

With organizations becoming more horizontal, it's not as obvious where one staff member starts and another begins. Find out who your go-to person is for critical needs.

Conversely, let them know how you can help them. Reinforce your value to the team in a helpful, service-oriented way.

And of course, the corollary to this notion is the Golden Rule. Be positive about others, and if you can't be positive, keep quiet.

I IS FOR INFORMED

Keep up with latest trends and best practices in your field. Network. Attend conferences, seminars and webinars. Know enough about a wide variety of donor relations functions to make thoughtful, well-informed decisions.

Go on site visits to similar organizations. Sometimes being in another work setting teaches you as much about who you are not as who you are. Search job postings. Even if you're not interested in applying for another job, it's a great way to learn what is going on in our field.

Though a Puritan heritage may say otherwise, there's nothing wrong in acknowledging that you're well versed in a particular field or subject matter. "Expert" comes from the Latin verb meaning to experience or try. So in a sense, we're all experts at what we've experienced. Assuming we learn from our actions, we can all stake a claim in being an expert in something! What are you an expert in? Name three things. Go.

O IS FOR ORGANIZATION

Learn how to organize your email. My email inbox contains only the items I need to follow up on. The rest are in electronic folders. Every six months, I clean out old folders. Control-F is no excuse for hoarding and cluttering.

Invest some time in establishing naming conventions so you can name documents in a way that they are easily recognized and retrieved. For instance, your resume should not be titled "resume.doc." Use initials, dates, document type – whatever it takes and makes the most sense.

Organization also means your institution. You should be fluent in facts and figures about your institution that donors or even the common person on the street would ask. How many students receive financial aid? How many beds are in your hospital? What types of art does your museum have in its permanent collection? What is your mission? Make sure you have your elevator speech down pat.

N IS FOR NOD

When you make a mistake, nod to yourself while saying this mantra: I own up to it, I will learn from it, and I will move on.

Nod your head. One, two, three. Repeat as necessary.

This is what responsible adults do: we acknowledge our role in a mistake, apologize, fix what we can and then get back to work. We do not blame others. We do not play victim, nor do we beat ourselves up. Fretting never helps. If you act immediately, sincerely, and positively, you will be seen as a person of character and strength rather than a goof.

S IS FOR STRENGTHS

Though I can't cite the source, I once read about a theory that says, "Rather than trying to improve your weaknesses, you're better off enhancing your strengths." It's all about return on investment.

Think about it in terms of sports. Say you stink at playing basketball, but you're better than average at football. Why would you spend all your time practicing basketball to get only marginally better, when you could devote your time entirely to football and get drafted into the NFL?

Apply that theory to work. Event planning is not my best skill, so I leave it to the experts. The event planners, in turn, ask my help in pulling data for the mailing lists and RSVPs. Should I work harder at planning events? Should they work harder at understanding data? I don't think so. I'd do better to keep pushing technology to improve their operations, and they should keep focusing on making each event better than the last. Two excellents > two mediocres.

To make RELATIONS ten characters long, I included an exclamation point, which stands for: YAY!!!

Forget about title and status. Choose a job that makes you go, "YAY!!!" If that's not the job you have, then find bits and pieces in that job that make you go, "YAY!!!" And if you still come up dry, volunteer or become active in a professional organization.

Go find your YAY!!! You deserve it and need it.

YAY!!! (DONOR) RELATIONS!

REROUTE THE TRAINS

DO YOU STEWARD GIFTS OR
CARE FOR YOUR DONORS?

For the past two nights, I've been more sleepless than usual. You see, I've been wrestling with this idea that struck me in a meeting and hasn't left yet. I am always asked what's the difference between donor relations now and 10 years ago or how to tell a high functioning shop apart from one that just goes through the motions. Well, my friends, I think I finally have my elevator speech answer.

> *The best and most sophisticated shops relate and
> care for donors, while the rest steward gifts.*

Some of you just paused for a moment to think, getting it instantly, some of you pawned this difference off as semantics, and yet others are still scratching their heads thinking, "Lynne, I haven't finished my coffee yet." Take it from a caffeine-free girl, it's not the coffee, it's the idea of it all. Can they be mutually exclusive?

I often say to my teammates and anyone else who will listen, "If it doesn't benefit the donor, we don't do it." And I think that demonstrates our donor-focus really well. But taking it a step further, I am now resonating with the question of not just why and who does it benefit, but are we stewarding the gift or caring for a donor?

I have a few examples to add to the debate. And yes, I am aware that in some instances, stewarding gifts can help us care for donors, but not really; not holistically. Being accountable is the right thing to do and, in many cases, a simple requirement.

It must go further. How does this nurture our relationship?

I have been on a violent crusade for years against gifts, plaques, and honor rolls. The reasons behind this attack of bayonets and battleships have been numerous and surface, but what I was failing to realize all along is that these types of efforts steward the gift and recognize it but don't holistically account for the humanness of the donor. I don't mean to go all philosophically militant here, but for me, it is a large shift in my worldview happening. It is a seismic synthesis of things that many of us have believed for years, explained in a manner that we can all grasp.

So besides physical gifts and recognition, what does this mean?

Let's take some events, like scholarship receptions or donor recognition receptions. We tell the donor we want to thank them, then we prescribe exactly how they will be thanked by us, and they better like it. Time, place, food, people, program, everything is dictated by us an of course their level of giving.

What if it was the other way around? One of our shop's greatest successes was a little postcard that thanked the donor for their impact and then invited them to campus when they were near to meet with those that benefit from their support. Donors ate it up, because it truly was about them, on their terms, and valued their relationship.

Let's also consider giving societies or gift clubs, the very nature of which is predicated on gift recognition, not donor caregiving. My value to a certain organization as a donor is dependent on my giving, not my volunteer involvement, closeness of relationship, years of involvement, or any other factor, just one shallow measure of my dedication, my wallet.

By now many of you are thinking I may not have taken my meds today, or mixed the blue and yellow pills. NOPE. I'm just thinking smarter. So what happens now?

Do we chuck all of the efforts we are making and start over? I wish it were that simple, but it's not. We have to reroute the trains, solve this problem, and effectively find a way to measure and build without predication on one shallow measure of a human, their gifts.

INFOGRAPHICS

COMMUNICATING WITH CONSTITUENTS

Lately, I have been seeing more and more clever uses for infographics and think that it is time for us to incorporate them into our communications.

Remember when you were in school and all of the kids didn't learn the exact same way? Some learned by reading, some by listening, some by doing, and some through viewing? This is the exact same principal to bring to our communications with our constituents. Infographics are dynamic ways to tell a complex story or deliver important information in a visual and engaging manner. They combine different learning and user absorption styles into one powerful message: yours.

But, I know what you're thinking: "Uhm, Lynne, I have a hard enough time coming up with good communication pieces? Why try this shiny new technique?"

I would challenge you to think that, just like in school, your constituents all see information and learn differently. Some of them will take the time to read that beautifully crafted story you want to tell them. Others either don't have the time or aren't interested in the narrative.

Think about it this way. Often we are asked to propose new ideas to our leadership. I can't tell you how many times I have seen evidence that the story isn't as important as the charts, statistics, and graphs that are so necessary for them and often left behind by us, too wrapped up in the emotional component and the message. Infographics bridge this for us with our constituents and can be a powerful tool.

So, how do you make an infographic of your own to incorporate into your communications? Your designers/ communications folks will be thrilled you are trying new methods and will be happy to work on the effort with you. Start simple, maybe using infographics we all grew up with, like a modified venn diagram or other familiar shape.

Then, challenge yourself, your teammates and your colleagues to get creative. There are many sources for inspiration out there! Remember, as we speed through our daily lives, both at work and at home, and data begins to overwhelm and overload us, it is our challenge to overcome this and make it easier and quicker for our constituents, to understand the need and impact of their giving.

Now, it's up to you to help tell the story.

CRISP, CLEAR, & CONCISE

TIPS TO MORE EFFICIENT COMMUNICATIONS

BY DEBBIE MEYERS

There is an old saying: If I'd had more time, I would have written less.

Think about how many emails you ignore because they look like they will take too much time to read. Long emails are disrespectful. Rather than the writer taking the time to be concise, the burden is on the reader to decipher what the note is all about. Delete. Next.

In newspapers, excess words cost money. The more words you use, the more likely you are to lose a reader and the less advertising space you have to sell. In cyberspace, wordiness can cost you reader attentiveness. Consider a 2008 study that showed the average web page visitor reads about 20 percent of the text. If your livelihood depends on people reading your website, you need to make your point succinctly.

So my point is less is better, if you keep your writing crisp, clear, and concise. Think about how you crop a picture. Cropping forces you to identify the main, important part of the image. It takes skill, patience, and creativity to crop your writing.

Here are a few suggestions and examples, with the disclaimer that these are guidelines, not absolutes. See if you can guess in each tip how I've discounted my own advice.

TIPS

ELIMINATE ALL UNNECESSARY WORDS

EXAMPLE
"We have seven *different* flavors."

Of course they're different. That's why there are seven of them.

EXAMPLE
"I love *both* my daughters and sons."

Not only is both unnecessary, it's unclear. Do you have only two daughters?

USE INTENSIFIERS AND ADVERBS SPARINGLY

EXAMPLE
one strong verb > a weak verb + adverb

sprint > run quickly

EXAMPLE
"I am so tired and very hungry."

When my mother packed to move, she wrote *Fragile* on nearly every box. Then she went to *Very Fragile* and *Extremely Fragile*. If everything is fragile, nothing is. If everything is very, nothing is. One teacher said to use *very* as you would *damn* – for emphasis only.

DON'T BE NEGATIVE

Besides being wordy, using negatives opens you to the risk of typing *now* instead of *not*. Moreover, people like to read positive, encouraging messages.

EXAMPLE
I am not able to attend.

Rather: I am unable to attend. (Avoid *not*.)

EXAMPLE
Don't run in the store, sweetheart.

Rather: Let's walk in the store, OK? (Be encouraging.)

AVOID "QUOTATION MARKS," ELLIPSES... (DON'T FORGET PARENTHESES) AND EXCLAMATION POINTS!

EXAMPLE
I don't want to be a "pest," but do you have that letter?

EXAMPLE
Going to the game will be fun (although I hope it doesn't rain).

These punctuation marks are at best unneeded and at worst distracting. Even if it's just for a second, the reader has to stop and figure out why they're there.

Exclamation points, by definition, mean you are exclaiming something. Be sure that when you use them, what you're writing is a big deal. Use them for dramatic effect, not mundane communication.

DO-OVERS

EXAMPLE 1

OLD
This is a system-generated report with regard to donors that have given $500 (soft-credit) or more during the previous week, including both primary and affiliated donors.

NEW

This system-generated report lists donors, including primary and affiliated, who have given at least $500 (soft-credit) during the previous week.

EXAMPLE 2

OLD

The information transmitted (including any attachments) is intended only for the person or entity to which it is addressed and may contain confidential and/or privileged material. Any review, retransmission, dissemination or other use of, or taking of any action in reliance upon, this information by persons or entities other than the intended recipient is prohibited. If you received this in error, please contact the sender and delete the material from any computer.

NEW

This email and any attachments are intended only for the addressee(s). If you received this email by mistake, please notify the sender and delete this message immediately, including attachments. If you are not the appropriate person to receive this message, distributing or reproducing it is prohibited.

EXAMPLE 3

OLD

After a student fills out this form, he or she needs to submit it to our office.

NEW

After students fill out this form, they need to submit it to our office. (Use plural. It's shorter and less awkward.)

Off my soapbox now. Wishing you success in your writing endeavors! And yes, I meant to use the exclamation point.

RESORTING TO FOOD BRIBERY

GETTING STUDENTS TO SHOW GRATITUDE

One of the wonderful things I love most about my career is that, in its finite end, I have helped students receive an education at some of the finest places of higher education this country has to offer. My current workplace is no exception. Although the tuition might be expensive to some, the value of the education these students receive is phenomenal.

A tiny disclosure here: when I was an undergraduate at South Carolina, I was a scholarship student. Without that support, I would not have been able to attend my alma mater, and be a proud alumna now, most thankful for four of the best years of my life and an education both in and out of the classroom that I know is priceless.

As most of the institutions I have worked for, approximately 70 percent of the students receive some sort of financial aid to underwrite their education, with most of this money being supplied by private donors to the University. And of course, my office, like many of yours, is directly responsible for reporting on these scholarships to donors and ensuring that they feel properly thanked and understand that their monies went to a great student who was much like them when they attended University.

The gap here comes in communicating this to the students. Don't get me wrong, at times I am overwhelmed by their stories, appreciative of their willing participation in the process of those who "get it" and understand that behind every dollar is a human being who believes so greatly in their education that they made it a philanthropic priority. My question to everyone out there reading is: what can we do about the rest of the recipients of these scholarships?

As I travel around the country and speak to others in my profession who work with scholarship or fellowship monies, this is one of the most consistent and troubling concerns I hear.

> "How do we get our students to respond to our requests for thank you notes?"

> "What ingenious techniques do you have for student participation in the process?"

These questions hit home to me on a daily, if not weekly, basis. I tell people often to go where the students are, educate and try to explain to them why these notes or gestures of gratitude are important. I am envious of my colleagues at institutions that are able to withhold funds from students until their cooperation is reached (wistful sigh).

But should we even have to go to these measures? I think the greater question here is: how do we educate those to truly be grateful and not feel entitled? I want to repeat here that I'm not talking about every student, I am talking about the ones who ignore my requests for thank you notes for their donor who is supplying them with a $25,000 scholarship, or those who call me and ask, "Do I *have* to write a note/meet with this donor?" I know for a fact that when they do meet their donors and tell their stories, there is a much deeper level of understanding.

But the question remains: how can I make that understanding happen if they refuse to communicate with me at all?

I don't want this to sound all gloom and doom. I have had amazing success at several institutions receiving wonderful thank you notes, calls, and meetings from a wide variety of students, but I realize now that the question is much larger: why is this work so difficult for us on the asking end and what can we do to find a solution?

So here are some tactics that have worked for me in the past.

- Find students where they are: Facebook, alternate emails, cell phones, cafeterias, soccer practice, etc.

- Don't be afraid to use the old guilt tactic; it works! Ask my mom!

- Resort to bribery if necessary; food is especially effective, cash works too.

- Put a face to the donors name, make the story personal.

- Use easy methods for submission, online, email, etc.

- Be persistent and consistent .If they think it is important to you it will be important to them!

- Obtain help from campus influencers, ie: financial aid, coaches, deans, professors, etc.

- Don't be afraid to engage the naysayers in a conversation and try to educate them about the process.

- Be thankful for the fabulous students who write tear jerking letters and who aren't afraid to wake up early to have breakfast with their donors.

- Realize that even though you are banging your head against a wall some days, you are doing good in the world. Sometimes that's enough.

WHEN IS ENOUGH ENOUGH?

FINDING THE GRATITUDE BALANCE

At a conference in Seattle, I had someone approach me, inferring that the leadership at his organization felt his donors were "thanked enough" and had reached a saturation point of gratitude. I immediately congratulated this individual, but was left with the nagging feeling that his leadership might have missed something along the way.

Not thirty minutes later, I was sitting with a friend musing over possible sessions for next year's conference when she told me of one of her teammates who writes such amazing thank you letters from leadership. They were so personal, so touching and sincere, that she often receives thank you letters in return.

So where is the balance? For me, I find it in the simplicity of sincerity. I have read far too many spirited and false emails and letters saying, "Thank You" with multiple explanation points and generic text to follow, something that, for me, falls on deaf ears.

I really believe we live gratitude and this comes through in our communications and our tone. I guess for me it's like a great John Coltrane performance, indulgent and filled with stories, saturated with emotion and intensity.

So when someone asks me if we can ever thank donors enough, I sit, sometimes melancholily, and think of all of the times that I am asked more than I receive and wonder if this can possibly be the case. We all have humble donors, we all have those who aren't. But at the core of the human experience is the need to feel valued and appreciated, whether it take one expression of gratitude or 56.

What we may fall victim to in our sincere attempt at appreciation is forcing fundraising constructs like namings and giving societies and other manufactured gratitude and recognition on a donor in a systematic approach to demonstrate gratitude. Sometimes the simpler the better, no need for a fancy label when a sincere touch will do.

Some donors desire nothing more than a sincere expression of intent, responsibility for the funds they entrust us with and the fulfilling role of attempting to make a difference. What nags at my soul is that if we are so successful at expressing gratitude, then why do only 27% of our donors stick around to experience it again. Data tells us its for a multitude of reasons, the most important is that we are constantly asking for more or asking period. As discussed in a previous chapter, our ask-to-thank ratio is all out of whack.

Imagine if you had a friendship like that; some of us do. Most of us have weeded out those "takers" by our thirties, because friends like that exhaust us, our resources and our patience in short order. Why would this be different from our donors?

It's one of those things that keeps me up at night, but as I travel and continue to meet more and more amazing fundraising professionals, I have the strong belief that while many of us are doing amazing things, gratitude can be more at the center, or core of our behaviors. Those that hold this ethos close are better fundraisers for it. I can't wait for the day when we can write a blog about the over-saturation of donor relations in fundraising. Until then, I think we have a ways to go and lots of us to help carry the gratitude forward.

THE BRIDESMAID DRESS

A THANK YOU THAT INCLUDES AN ASK?!

Lately, I've been on the receiving end of some pretty confusing donor communications from non-profits and universities. I get a pretty envelope with the words *Thank You* printed on the front in appropriate colors. I giddily open the envelope, expecting an amazing donor relations piece and a sincere thank you and then BOOM! I'm smacked upside the head with a solicitation. NOT COOL!

I am a strong proponent that a thank you should be pure, sincere, and unadulterated, and a solicitation should have nice appreciative language, but the two should not form some mutant species like the liger. Let's face it, some things have only one purpose in life.

Take the humble bridesmaid dress for example. No matter how much the sales clerk and your soon to be married friend try to convince you, no piece of that "apple green" or "lavender" taffeta or organza is getting near your body again for another purpose. You might as well have just set that $300 on fire. You're NOT going to wear it again for a "special occasion." It will just sit there in your closet and taunt you, saying, "You could have had a vacation." Bridesmaid dresses are like asks; just let them be what they are. Don't sew a fake flower on them and pretend that it is what it isn't. It's a solicitation, not a thank you. Keep the lines clean and clear.

The THASK, it's a *real* problem. The same goes for a solicitation and a thank you:

> *Dear Aunt Shirley,*
>
> *Thank you so much for the cabbage patch doll, valued at $49.99. I will love Xavier and hug him and keep his clothes nice and clean. I really appreciate my birthday present. I am, however, growing older and I think that Rainbow Brite is the next hot thing. Christmas is coming, what do you say, send me one of those?*
>
> *See you next year,*
>
> *Lynne*

This is just as tacky as tacking a solicitation to an ask. It may be an exaggerated version of reality, but how many of us have received a thank you letter or receipt with a reply device in it? And then we professionals wonder why first time donor retention levels are so low.

2 + 2 = 4... most of the time. Remember the #1 reason donors stop giving is because they are over-solicited. Let's cut them a break and decide that we're JUST going to sincerely thank them and tell them the impact of their gift, *without* shoving a link to the giving website or a reply device down their throats.

So just like picking the perfect bridesmaid dress, don't go down without a fight! Keep on advocating for your donors and remember that the most sincere and meaningful thing we can do is to thank someone.

Sometimes, simplicity is best.

PART 3

THE PRACTICE OF DONOR RELATIONS

GIFT DOCUMENTATION

ARE EXCEPTIONS THE RULE?

BY DEBBIE MEYERS

The past several years, I have drafted gift documentation for new funds. At my disposal were these tools:

1. A checklist submitted by the gift officer outlining the fund particulars– fund name fund and purpose, donor, donor motivation, payment method and schedule, award criteria

2. A gift document handbook, sort of a cook book for fund agreements

3. 3Templates and language for endowed, expendable, capital and deferred gifts

4. Old agreements

Everything I need is all right there in black and white, right?

Just like a manual on how to raise a child or guide to building an atom bomb.

Just as in raising kids or building bombs, when it comes to documenting gifts, the exception is becoming the rule.

Templates are only a starting point. Thus, because we often find ourselves in uncharted territory, it's more important than ever to make sure that your agreements are accurate, precise and functional. Below are three common pitfalls and a suggested ounce of prevention.

INACCURATE INFORMATION

Not everyone is a stickler for detail. One gift officer spelled his $1.5 million donor's name with every variation of capitalization, spacing and punctuation: bin Al Shanu, Bin Al-Shanu, bin al Shanu (fictional name). Another transposed his donor's first and middle names. The agreement got up the food chain for signature and when the error was discovered, I had to take the hit.

Prevention: Regardless of who's at fault, the buck stops with the agreement author. Assume nothing, verify everything.

PAYMENT VEHICLES

Donors use sophisticated payment methods these days: donor-advised funds, matching gifts, their family foundations. The IRS will recognize only one legal donor, and John Donor can't pay off his personal pledge through money he gave to Fidelity.

Prevention: Teach your gift officers to proactively ask donors how they intend to pay. Also, review the donor's record to see if previous payments came through any of these vehicles. Determining the legal donor can affect who gets the receipt and acknowledgment, so do what you can to avoid surprises at tax time.

UNREALISTIC EXPECTATIONS

Donors, particularly scholarship donors, have good intentions...and you know how the first part of that saying goes. Some like the idea of a committee picking the winner of a student essay contest – a method that's cumbersome and impossible to monitor. Some want to pick the recipient themselves, award it to an athlete or reward a student "of good moral character." Last I saw, our admissions form doesn't have a checkbox for good or bad moral character.

Prevention: To avoid having donors ask us to administer their funds in ways that are illegal, impractical or downright impossible, provide continuing education with your gift officers to make them aware of current laws, admissions procedures (if you're in higher ed) and IRS standards that enable them to walk donors through the right paths at the outset. Create internet sites or publications that clearly outline your policies, for gift officers and donors.

A more philosophical pitfall I've run up against lately is the legalese rhetoric we use in our agreements – and I mean the Universal We, because I have yet to see a warm and fuzzy version of a gift agreement.

Ironically, gifts we deem important (large) enough to document can sound cold and off-putting to our biggest donors. Agreement can sound more like a contract than an acknowledgment of our gratitude and their intentions.

The problem, I think, is that many gift agreements and template language are like surf-and-turf or sleeper sofas – you get the worst of both, the best of neither. We try to document our gratitude to the donor then get into the legal housekeeping of when they're going to pay and what happens if...

BLOOD DIAMONDS

DO YOU HAVE MORALITY CLAUSES?

UCLA gave $425,000 back to a donor: his name was Donald Sterling. Some of you may be surprised; I applaud them.

(For those not in the know, Donald Sterling, is a former NBA owner who was banned from the league for life after, among other things, recordings of him making racist comments were made public.)

This is the best of us. This is the other side of stewardship. It is protecting our organization from donors who do not have the best intentions.

In this light, I ask you, does your organization have a morality clause in its gift agreements? If you don't, I worry for you. Take it from the "Olivia Pope" of fundraising; I'm often called in by organizations to help them fix the messes. One simple clause would have helped them avoid this. Having a gift acceptance committee can also help avoid accepting gifts from those with questionable funding sources or backgrounds.

Did you know that at some universities there once was a Kenneth Lay Chair of Ethical Business?

Would you accept a gift from someone who made their money from blood diamonds? From international slavery?

From illegitimate business practices? It's no longer safe to think this won't happen to you. The names Madoff, Petters, Lay and others have become common embarrassments for organizations and there are other names you probably have never heard of.

Yes, this is important to us and should be. We're not the morality police, but we must protect our organizations from undue risk. Most non-profits depend on public goodwill to attract donors. Close association with someone whose name has been badly tarnished can taint the nonprofit's reputation and harm its ability to attract support.

Here is some sample language to have reviewed by your general counsel and then have in place in your gift agreements:

> *If at any time the donor or his or her name may compromise the public trust or the reputation of the institution, including acts of moral turpitude, the institution, with the approval of the Board of Trustees, has the right to remove the name or return the gift.*

Please heed my advice; it is much easier to do something up front, than take retroactive action.

SURVEY MONKEYS

HOW TO KNOW WHAT
YOUR DONORS WANT

I am constantly being asked to help people come up with ideas and plans to help steward their donors. Last week alone, I fielded requests for designing a high end gift society to creating a stewardship plan in detail from scratch. Each time I receive a blanket request like this or read an obtusely vague question on one of the listservs, the first question that pops into my mind is always, "Have you asked your donors what they want?"

In reality, I can give you some generalizations based on trends, some emerging ideas and other ideas that I have proven successful over time at different institutions. However, what I cannot produce, without time and research is exactly what will work for your donor base and population. I have found that far too often, we as donor relations professionals spend too much time planning for what we think donors will want, without even asking them first!

Every time I go to a consulting job, one of the most important meetings for me as I do my analysis is to have dinner with a group of highly engaged donors and volunteers. I learn so much from them and, while generally their needs are similar, most times they vary widely.

This brings me to a hot topic I've been dealing with lately: surveying. How many of you survey your donors, formally or informally? Why? Why NOT? It is a wonderful, cost effective way to receive feedback from your target audience. It also allows for wonderful substantiation of your work to leadership and key decision makers. It also will greatly aid your strategic planning efforts. So here are a few examples of surveying your donors, followed by some links to actual surveys from organizations.

1. Use Survey Monkey/online surveying following an event or new initiative, not just to those who participated, but also to those that didn't. What motivated them not to?

2. Send a survey included with your endowment or annual reports asking them if the information was clear, if there is more they need from you, who else should receive this in the future, and also if you can send it digitally in PDF from now on!

3. Arrange a small focus group of donors and volunteers, perhaps over lunch to talk about how they feel your organization treats them after they give. Make sure this group includes a sample of your donors, not just major givers, and all ages too!

4. Make phone calls to spot-check how things are going, informal, yet informative!

RETAIL VALUE OF MY CABBAGE PATCH DOLL

WHY RECEIPTS & ACKNOWLEDGMENTS ARE NOT THE SAME

The subject of receipts and acknowledgments comes up many times a week on discussion boards, listservs and other development forums. So I decided to give you my definitive perspective, my opinion on the receipt and acknowledgment issue. Again, this is my opinion but I speak with donors quite frequently and will add anecdotes as needed to further my argument.

A receipt is a systematized document prepared in a mechanical and transactional way that allows the donor to use it for tax or other business purposes. It may (read *should*) have language of gratitude on it, but in no means should supplant or replace a proper thank you letter (aka, acknowledgment). Think of it this way: you're at a restaurant and you get the bill for dinner, you pay it and are left with a receipt. It may have nice language on it like "Thanks for your business" or "See you soon," but it is a receipt for a transaction and people keep it for their records. The reason a good receipt is beautiful and not so dry is because if this is the one thing they keep from their donation, I want it to be branded and have visual impact along with pertinent information.

An acknowledgment is a thank you note, albeit on nice stationery with an official seal most of the time. It boils down to a thank you note. Thank you notes should *never* have the amounts listed in them anywhere. The core reason I don't believe that a thank you note and receipt should be combined comes from the old Emily Post ideals my mother instilled in me. For example, when you receive a gift, you thank you note should *not* read:

> *Dear Grandmother, I just received your Birthday present and am thrilled. The blonde blue-eyed Cabbage Patch doll, currently valued at $49.99 retail, is great and I am sure I will play with it and think of you. Thank you for thinking of me.*

Doesn't sound quite right now does it? That's because it's not! Note here it also *doesn't* sound right in the note to ask for another gift:

> *Grandmother, I also have a great need for some Rainbow Brite dolls, something I know you understand and are passionate about.*

Gag. But how many times have I received a receipt or thank you letter from a philanthropic organization with another ask. It's sad, and sounds desperate.

Why am I harping on this? Because so often we get it wrong. Donors, now more than ever, are giving small test gifts to see how your organization will treat them; I hear it time and time again. Send them just a receipt and you can plan on being ignored by them the next time around. *Every* gift, no matter the amount, deserves a thank you, no matter the form, in addition to their receipt.

This past week I was fortunate enough to attend a donor panel and we asked them about acknowledgments and receipts. Their answer was resounding and clear, send a receipt because they need it for accountants and such, but they also expect a thank you. At higher levels, the interesting fact was that they didn't mind a template letter. They don't expect campus presidents to hand write all of their notes and they are savvy enough to know we write them anyway. What they did note as meaningful and desired is if the VP, President, etc just jotted them a short note saying "Hello" or Thank you" at the bottom of the template letter. This is what they want and what they need.

Frankly, as much as we toil over our letters and stress over their wording and length, the tragic truth remains; they end up in the trash. I'm still looking for the donor who keeps all of my hard written acknowledgment template letters in a hand carved box next to his or her bed and rereads them nightly or so. It just doesn't happen in the real world, but they all keep the receipts. Spend some more time and energy there to make sure they convey information in a meaningful and responsible way. Receipts are focused on a particular transaction or gift, while acknowledgments are focused on the donor.

So the moral of the story is that, much like stewardship and donor relations, the words receipt and acknowledgment are not interchangeable. If they were, they'd be the same word.

INSTITUTIONAL RESPONSE TO A GIFT

BEST PRACTICES: ACKNOWLEDGMENTS

BY DEBBIE MEYERS

Whether you are creating, enhancing, or reviewing your acknowledgment protocol, the process is often overwhelming.

All the questions that buzz around our heads!

Who should sign the letters? At what level? Hand sign or machine sign? Does it need to be a letter? Do we acknowledge pledges? Do we treat corporate gifts differently from individuals – because, really, does the Australian Chicken Council (real life example) find a letter from our president meaningful?

Our standard go-to solution is to benchmark our peers. Often we have no choice – our well-meaning, but sometimes less-than-imaginative, decision-makers require us to see what our "aspirational and inspirational" (don't ya just love a good buzz phrase?!) peers are doing.

Benchmarking, as I've noted before, has its limitations. And for acknowledgments, in particular, I would say benchmarking is irrelevant. What is relevant are a number of factors that can help guide you toward a reasonable system.

Climb up to the top of the mountain and look out over your institution. Get a firm grasp of the big picture that is uniquely your institution. What do you see?

Ask yourself: What does you institution consider a major gift?

If your president is signing letters for $2,000 gifts to the annual fund and your major gift level starts at $100,000, something's off. It's not that $2,000 gifts aren't important. They are. I would LOVE for someone to give me $2,000! And they should be acknowledged.

But having your organization's leader sign letters for gifts at too low of a level can create a negative perception about your organization and *sense of entitlement among lower-level donors*. If everyone is special, no one is special. Moreover, a form letter from the president with a digital signature is practically meaningless and borders on junk mail. So how do you know where to draw the line?

Check your data – How many gifts at which levels does your institution receive over a year?

You can't blindly set up levels for acknowledgments without knowing how many letters you're talking about. You need context. If your president has only enough time to hand write 10 cards a week, then see at what level those topten are.

Then ask: What kind of leader and staff resources do you have?

Does your chancellor enjoy handwriting notes? Is your president willing to devote the time it takes to write the number of thank-you's you want? Will your CEO sit on letters until they're hopelessly out of date? Do you have adequate staff to carefully research each gift and donor to craft a letter that will get framed and hung on a wall? Or do you have one person whose duties include 50 things, among them presidential correspondence?

Are other departments also doing acknowledgments?

Find out if other departments, colleges, schools, or units within your organization are sending letters, to whom and under what conditions. That information will help you avoid holes in the overall process.

Armed with big picture information, let's look at a more detailed plan by plugging in these factors:

1. Gift amount – identify the natural groupings, breaks, and cutoffs.

2. Gift type – choose what you'll acknowledge: cash, pledges, pledge payments, on-line gifts.

3. Gift allocation – find out which are already being acknowledged or those needing to be covered centrally.

4. Donor affiliation – label the groups receiving special or different treatment, like VIPs, trustees, major donors, first-time donors and corporations/foundations.

5. Medium – determine your delivery method: email, phone call, hand-signed form letter, electronic signature form letter, individualized hand-signed letter, handwritten note

Then add in two key guiding principles:

- The best acknowledgments come from the person/ entity benefiting most directly from the gift.

- Acknowledgments are an institutional response to a gift. To be effective, they must be timely, accurate and sincere.

Acknowledgments are an art and a science. The science of timeliness and accuracy are mechanical functions that you will iron out with your IT and data management colleagues. The art of sincerity comes through not only in the language, which should be refreshed frequently, but through the person signing the letter. A thank-you from a person who has little to no connection to the gift will not be as sincere as one from someone who directly benefits from it.

Considering your criteria factors and guiding principles, you're ready to create a grid or hierarchy for your acknowledgments.

Start at the top. Given the volume of letters, your resources and leader's availability, determine who will get a leadership acknowledgment. For instance, a board member who gives $5,000 will probably qualify because of affiliation, even though you set the dollar level at $100,000. Document any criteria that make sense for your institution and your top leader. Then, for everything else...

Divide and conquer.

A staff of two cannot effectively manage sending out 10,000 letters a year. So weigh and balance a reasonable workload, playing off quality vs. quantity, which often translates into timeliness vs. personalization. Which is better – a timely and accurate form letter, or an eloquent personalized letter that arrives a month after the gift is made? Figure out where you want to draw your line in the sand.

Then find the holes for allocation. Who would acknowledge $10,000 unrestricted gifts (no dean, not high enough for the president)? Can you eliminate on-line gifts under a certain threshold by simply replying with an electronic acknowledgment? (Yes, you can and should.)

Many institutions have the VP for development sign second-tier gifts. Depending on your staff resources and how strongly our VP feels about it, you may want to re-think that strategy. At a university, for example, if thebusiness school dean acknowledges gifts of $1,000 and higher, and your president acknowledges $50,000 and up, you can be reasonably confident that the $10,000 business school donor will get a letter from the business dean and really could care less (in many cases) about a form letter from a VP for advancement, whose job it is to raise moneyand has no direct stake in the welfare of the business school. (See Guiding Principal #1.)

The process and rules are not going to be the same for every institution. To paraphrase Dr. Seuss, no one is you-er than you. Using the information and theory you gain through this process, you should be able to create a meaningful, effective acknowledgment system that would make even Penelope Burk proud!

PLEDGE FULFILLMENT RATES

DOES YOUR PLEDGE REMINDER HELP?

As I searched for samples of amazing pledge reminders, I was sorely disappointed with what I found. Many of our pledge reminders treat reminding donors that they still have a commitment to fulfill as routine and mindless as when the cable company sends an overdue notice.

What does this say to our donors? It makes the entire effort not to have our relationships be entirely transactional just that, a business transaction. After all of our work to retain donors and realizing that national donor retention hovers around 27%, what is our national pledge fulfillment rate? Do you know how many of your organization's pledges are written off at the end of every fiscal year?

If you don't know the answers, it may be time to find out. If you haven't seen your pledge reminder and thought about the way it makes your donors feel about their giving, it is time you had a look. Does it arrive, in the mail in a windowed envelope with a slip of paper that is no more friendly than the water bill? What kind of messaging is enclosed?

I understand that pledge reminders need to be somewhat automated and easy to produce, but why do they have to be so ugly and lacking in impact or gratitude? It goes back to the theory that servers in restaurants are trained to write you a hand written note on the bill, it increases their tips exponentially, what if we applied that theory to pledge reminders? We know they need to convey the information that there is an outstanding payment, but could we include information on what gifts like the pledge were able to do? Could we say thank you? Could we at least have a softer "landing" than, "This is what you owe"?

Donor relations is everywhere and is inextricable from the giving experience. However, donor relations sometimes has little or no input on these documents.

We should. We must. We need to.

It is imperative that at all times we convey gratitude and impact to our donors, not just that the transaction is incomplete.

TACKY RECEIPTS

WHAT DOES YOUR GIFT RECEIPT SAY ABOUT YOUR ORGANIZATION?

As I ran a ton of errands this weekend, one of my stops was my local Walgreens for a few miscellaneous items. As I left the store, purchases nestled snugly in my granny cart, the clerk handed me a small novela of receipts. There was one that was just an ad for something I purchased, one was a coupon hoping I'd buy another item, and then the register receipt that was the length of my body. Good grief! As I pondered the waste, thinking about how I hated paper and only kept receipts when the IRS tells me I have to, I thought about our receipts that we send as organizations and what they say about us.

Have you looked at your receipt lately? Is it easy to read and colorful? Does it share your mission and have a message of gratitude? Are you wasting the back of it with empty space?

Remember, the tax receipt is one of the only items of print a donor will ever keep. What kind of lasting impression will you have with them? When they look at it during tax time will they smile or frown?

A well done receipt doesn't have to be overly complicated, but it does have to be clear, direct and responsible. Receipts don't need to overwhelm with information. Keep it simple.

Also, please don't forget a receipt's purpose. It is a tax document and a quick way to let the donor know we have received their gift. It should leave your office within 24-48 hours of the receipt of the gift; no exceptions.

Please don't include a BRE or another ask in with the receipt, that's tacky. Give your donors room to breathe before you re-solicit them, you may even want to thank them, too!

Also, don't forget to receipt responsibly. If someone has set up a reoccurring or monthly gift, don't send them a receipt every time; one at the end of the calendar year is sufficient. Additionally, give them the option to receive their receipts digitally should that be their preference.

QUID PRO QUO: OH NO!

TOKEN GIFTS AND DONOR RELATIONS

Last week a hot topic flew across the listservs that I am a member of. Yesterday, I brought it to my home base listserv to the surprise and sometime delight of some of my professional colleagues across the land. The IRS has just released its section 526 ruling for this year. And lo and behold, there in tax-ease for all of us to misinterpret is a stricter ruling on the giving of "token gifts" to donors.

The quid pro quo benefit limits for have just been announced by the IRS. They are as follows (please check your current year's document):

> For gifts IN EXCESS OF $49.50, you may provide insubstantial (token) items, containing the organization name or logo, without reducing the gift amount as long as the cumulative low-cost value is LESS THAN $9.90.

> For gifts below $49.50, you must fully disclose the value of all such benefits - and reduce the gift accordingly - if that benefit value is less than $1.

> Below that gift level the token benefit exclusion no longer applies.

> Therefore, for a gift of $25, the highest cumulative FMV of benefits you can provide without having to disclose/

reduce the gift is a whopping 50 cents. A $10 gift = 20 cents in benefits without disclosure.

For more substantial benefits, like events not items, you do not have to disclose the value as long as the cumulative value of all benefits does not exceed $99 or 2% of the amount given - whichever is LESS.

This is why, on every solicitation some organizations send, they include a check box for: "Please waive benefits so we can deduct the full amount of donation for tax purposes."

The "receipt" of the benefit does not have to be at the exact second the gift is made – getting it in the mail or in person a few weeks or months later as a direct result of a gift means that the donor "receives something in exchange." These limits are right on trend and have made many of us in the donor relations world that abhor tchotchkes very happy.

But for many of my colleagues, the panicked question remains, "I'm supposed to follow these rules!?!" The answer is simply YES.

Not only are we stewards of donors funds and the builders of relationships, but we are also their advocates. Think of us as nurses in this sense; whatever is best for the patient/donor we *must* advocate for. This includes helping to protect them from losing their deductibility of their gift because we just *had* to give them another pen set. We must advocate and ensure that these IRS rules are followed to the letter.

I think from an internal perspective, this means a sit down with your counsel and having them make a definitive ruling on this tax code for your organization. The next step involves your communicating with your internal constituents and explaining this to them. Making sure that they understand that this isn't just an idea you came up with so you can get rid of that closet full of gifts in your office (*ahem*). Complete understanding and compliance is a must; it is our pleasure and duty to at all times keep the donor in mind.

According to Penelope Burk, who I will quote here, this directly aligns with what donors are telling her repeatedly in her studies and jives with what some of us have been preaching for years. Donor relations is not about an exchange of money for items or perks; it is a relationship building, appreciative, strategic, and holistic view of a relationship.

Penelope says:

> *On this issue, both the IRS and donors are in complete agreement. Donors don't want these token gifts and sending them makes fundraisers' jobs much more difficult, especially in tough economic times. Why give donors one more reason to question the cost-effectiveness of fundraising appeals and the sincerity of not-for-profits who solicit with a sense of urgency, then refund some of the donor's gift in the form of a trinket that they never asked for and don't want.*
>
> *There are, however, gifts that are truly appreciated by donors, which positively contribute to their retention and higher gift value, and which have no negative implication. They are:*
>
> - *Beautiful, original thank you letters -- considered to be the ultimate in donor recognition and often referred to by donors as "gifts";*
>
> - *Thoughtful, impromptu calls that acknowledge a recent gift or simply the ongoing loyalty of a donor – stunningly effective at furthering donor retention, a source of tremendous information about donors for the purpose of cultivating them into major giving, and highly effective as a motivator for volunteers and paid professional fundraisers, reminding them why they do this job.*
>
> *It's not often that I am able to say that the IRS got it right, but they certainly have on this issue. They are doing the fundraising industry and, in particular, our stewardship profession, a favor.*

GIVING SOCIETIES

HOW TO DO THEM WELL

There was a wonderful donor panel populated by some generous philanthropists who also were great characters. We really enjoyed listening to them tell about their relationships with giving, etc.

At one point an attendee stood up and asked the panel how they felt about giving societies and which ones they belonged to. The grande dame of the panel grabbed the mic and said soundly, "Well, I am a proud member of the International Floral Designers and the Elite Floral Designers of America." Everyone in the room zoomed around, and glances were caught, while most of us were thinking that her "miss" of this development question brought home an important point: most donors don't know that they belong to a giving club or society that we have created, manufactured and branded for them.

We spend countless hours discussing giving societies on listservs and at conferences, and yet I have never heard a donor say that they increase their giving or give so they can be a member of a giving society. My friend Paige went to great lengths to redefine her giving societies at Carnegie Mellon and has had much success with them. She simplified them and made sure that for every one she created, she had meaningful benefits that met the donors needs.

How many of you can name all of your giving societies and why they are each important and what benefits are received? I didn't think so. I think giving societies are often over-hyped and under-staffed, with many levels and confusion about what exactly it means. So the question then is how do you do them well? Here are some of my tips:

1. Don't create one if you don't have a clearly defined purpose or goal and know that this vehicle will work for your donors. What's wrong with just stewarding them well without giving it a fancy name and logo?

2. Keep it simple. I have three societies, two of which are currently working well and one which I am developing. A million dollar plus cumulative giving society, a planned giving society, and coming next, a consecutive giving society similar to the Carolina Circle.

3. If you delve into societies, make sure you have the time and resources to do so. Under-promise and over-deliver; the reverse can be tragic. Nothing is worse than a splashy launch and not having a good product to back it up; anyone remember Pepsi Clear?

4. Be very careful about your benefits and quid pro quo IRS laws, CASE standards, etc. Make sure you get your list reviewed by legal so you're not digging yourself a ditch.

5. This related back to a practice I always employ: survey your donors first and find out what is important to them. Does a society matter to them? What are their needs?

6. Make sure that you make the number of people in each society manageable, ensuring that if they are to get something hand-signed by your president or CEO, that it indeed is possible. Exclusivity doesn't mean thousands of people getting the same thing.

7. For the love of all that is good in the world, stay away from items/tchotckes. One caveat, I have seen lapel pins and nametag identifiers used well. Items cause tax problems, logistical and shipping issues, and donors don't give to get. What is most meaningful to them is personalized notes, insider access, and clear communication.

YOUR 3RD GRADE BIRTHDAY PARTY

BE INCLUSIVE OF DONORS

Hang with me here, folks, as I walk you through a nice little metaphor. Remember 3rd grade? Or have your tried to block out the year of long division? I remember 3rd grade, I had a great birthday party planned, the good old roller skating party. I was so excited for the event with my friends until my mother dropped the hammer: I had to invite everyone in my class, even the girl that pushed me off of the slide so she could go first, with me falling off and breaking my wrist, hrmph. I digress, my mother, as usual, was right, I had to invite everyone to the party.

When you think of donor recognition and giving societies, I want you to think of my mother...uhm, I mean...I want you to be inclusive. Our donors deserve to be valued and included in the things we do to recognize and thank them. Here are a few examples.

YOUR PLANNED GIVING SOCIETY

How is your list compiled? How do people gain access to the society benefits? I personally and professionally believe that if a person tells you or someone in your development office that they have included you in their life planning, invite them to the party. Revocable, irrevocable, bequest, annuity, CLUT, CRUT, who cares? These people have shown a dedication to us and we should be grateful and show appreciation. What's one more on the guest list? For those of you shuddering in fear, there have been no widespread reports, or any for that matter, of the elderly faking planned gifts just to come to a cocktail party or to obtain your car decal. Deep breaths. Treat them right, be inclusive and reap the rewards.

YOUR LONGEVITY/LOYALTY SOCIETY

How are you pulling that list? If I have to give to you 5 or more fiscal years in a row, I might fall off and be excluded. But if you pull the list by calendar and by fiscal year, I will probably hit the mark and be grateful for the inclusion. Remember, donors don't mark our fiscal year on their calendars in large red letters like we do. And, it's about them, not us.

Also, for those of you with established societies, run a list of donors who have missed a year or two for eligibility and offer them the opportunity to buy those years back. Georgia Tech does this with great success. Try it, your annual fund folks will love you for the partnership!

YOUR ANNUAL AND CUMULATIVE AMOUNT SOCITIES

For both your annual amount and cumulative amount societies, do you count matching gifts and soft credit? No? Why not? The donors had to fill out a form in paper or online to help you get the money, why shouldn't they receive recognition credit? Remember, our job is one of inclusiveness and appreciation, the more the merrier. We have an opportunity to shine for these folks, to demonstrate their true value to us and to show them our appreciation for all of their efforts.

Back to the metaphor at hand. Our job as I see it boils down to all of the things my mom did so well at my birthday parties: make everyone feel welcome, thank them for all of their gifts (even the Playdough that she wouldn't allow anywhere near the carpet), make sure everyone gets a slice of pizza and cake, (even the annoying kid that had to have the corner piece with the most frosting or didn't eat pepperoni), to make sure the party favors were the best ever and made lots of noise (tchotchkes be damned), and to make sure that at the end of the day, everyone had a great, memorable time.

Make sure your donors are treated the same way a birthday girl is, and that they remember that extra touch as memorably as I do.

THE THANK-A-THON

TIPS AND IDEAS TO DO YOUR OWN

What's a thank-a-thon? Think the exact opposite of a phone-a-thon: student callers make calls for hours on end, just to thank donors, nothing less than an honest and sincere expression of gratitude!

I have implemented this wherever I go and think it is one of the best investments of time, effort, and money an organization can do. Calling donors just to say thanks is a magical thing; they're always waiting for the other shoe to drop, awaiting an ask. Surprise! There isn't one! The students love it, too, because they get to express appreciation to those that have supported them directly.

So here are some tips and ideas for how to conduct your own thank-a-thon!

SEGMENT WISELY

We used 5 segments and ordered them in priority: scholarship donors, donors of 10 or more consecutive calendar years at any amount, mid-level donors, first time givers, and those in our top giving society of $1 million plus lifetime cumulative.

WRITE THANK YOU SCRIPTS

Separate thank you scripts were written for each group and placed at the top of the color coded sheet, with spaces for whether or not they reached someone, voicemail, or bad number and a comments section.

RECOGNIZE THE IMPORTANCE OF EMAIL

I used this opportunity to acquire emails, and so anyone with a blank email was asked to provide one so we could thank them digitally!

Follow up with those we couldn't reach or left a voicemail with will be digitally sent email thank yous with photos of the student callers.

INVITE STAFF AND ADMINISTRATION TO JOIN

Although I was unable to do it this year, in years past at other organizations, I have invited staff, faculty, senior administration, and trustees to join in and have done a reverse pyramid thank-a-thon. Students call the biggest donors with people like the president of the university or trustees calling first time donors or loyalty donors. Imagine making a first time gift of $25 and getting a call from the chairman of the board! It's magical!

MAKE PROPER ACKNOWLEDGEMENT

For those consecutive givers, I always put how many years they have given, so try and acknowledge properly. It is amazing how that special touch goes such a long way!

NEVER MAKE AN ASK

That doesn't mean we don't raise money. This year, in two nights, we pulled in an additional $25,000 from people who were overwhelmed by the simple act of being thanked. Who says stewardship doesn't make money?

UPDATE YOUR DATA

The data acquired from these calls is valuable and is immediately updated in our database, from numbers that no longer work, to new spouses or, unfortunately, people who have passed on. It is a wonderful way to help cull information!

SO WHAT ARE THE DOWNSIDES?

As you reinforce a culture of gratitude at your organization, there will be questions from donors and awkward pauses while they wait for you to make an ask that never happens, but in reality it is win-win on all sides. Student phone-a-thon callers see what it's like to be grateful, and donors are delighted by the simple act of thankfulness.

RECYCLING TCHOTCKES

6 INNOVATIVE WAYS TO BE THANKFUL

Allow me to share with you some innovative yet cost friendly ways to thank your donors.

HAVE OTHERS STOP AND RECOGNIZE THOSE WHO GIVE SO MUCH

Many of you have installed thank-a-donor weeks at your organizations, with great success I am happy to report! Make sure those outside of your development office are aware and help you thank your donors, getting a note from those who benefit from your support is priceless.

SET UP A SKYPE BOOTH IN YOUR OFFICE

Here's what you need: a banner or sheet or some type of wall covering, a computer or tablet or phone with Skype installed and some willing staff or volunteers. We have our students call their scholarship donors who are far away even international ones and offer to Skype with them so they can see the face behind their philanthropy.

It is widely successful and popular. Students are teaching donors, if they already don't know, how to use Skype and the interactions are fabulous. What a pleasant surprise if this happened once a month! It is completely donor-focused, scheduled around them, at their time and convenience, unlike events.

RECYCLE OR DONATE THOSE TCHOTCKES YOU'VE BEEN WANTING TO

Go ahead, they serve no purpose. Allow your key volunteers or donors amazing experiences instead. Have them attend a rehearsal, have them "conduct" your band, give them inside access to your organization, have them meet others who volunteer, nominate them for an award, write a blurb about them for their local newspaper. The point is, do something!

WRITE NOTES TO YOURSELF

Ok, this one is good. Go get a notecard, piece of paper, etc. and write yourself a note of the things you're proud of, grateful for, or dreams you may have. Self-address it and give to someone else and ask them to send it to you in a month or two. Remember, gratitude and acknowledgment is something we don't often give ourselves, so force your own hand at it today. You'll thank me later.

RECONNECT IMPACTFUL STORIES

Take the time to ask your constituents, either by phone, email, or better yet, social media, someone who had an impact on them. It could be anyone, a certain professor or staff member, a mentor, or even the guy at the cafeteria who always remembers you like blueberry pancakes on Wednesdays, and listen to their story. Then make it your mission to reconnect those two and then share their story everywhere you can. Stories like that are powerful and profound, and frankly we need more good news like that daily. As for me, I'm going to write the two professors that changed my life today at lunch.

MAKE YOUR OWN CONTRIBUTION

Finally, now that you've done all of that, you should have some leftover money in your budget...ha! I would ask you to pick one volunteer or donor a month and make a contribution to a cause they care about or a fund they have with your organization. Giving is the best gift. Philanthropy is the type of behavior that loves to be replicated. If you want to truly thank a donor, thank them in kind, not with items or stuff they can buy, but by giving. It doesn't have to be a significant gift, just one that honors them and their spirit.

THE BEST DONOR GIFT MONEY CAN BUY

GIVE THEM SOMETHING THEY CAN'T GET

If it is not clear to you by now, I absolutely abhor tchotchkes for donor recognition and am thrilled when the IRS clamps down on giving for Quid Pro Quo sake. As many of you know, most people of means have most things that money can buy, and if they can order it like you can, there is no point in giving them an item with your logo on it.

What many of our donors long for and need are experiences that money can't buy. For me, that involves having them meet and converse with those that benefit from their funds: students and faculty. Other than a memory, they aren't left with much.

I am actually asking you to spend some money, gasp! And here is the most meaningful gift you can give donors that time and time again they avow to love: personal, custom picture books. These books take time and effort, but they document a real tangible interaction that cannot be easily duplicated. They're beautiful, hard-bound, and completely custom. And, they can be had for an affordable price. Most of these books can be purchased for anywhere from $20-$40 depending on size, pages, and your Internet couponing ability.

There are many providers out there. We use blurb.com and in the past have used snapfish.com with great results. There are others, but I find these two to be the best. They are easy to use, arrive in a couple of weeks and make the best donor gifts ever. They are unique, something that can't be bought at a store, and better yet, tell a great story. Our donors love to have them in their homes as conversation pieces and we use them for every honoree at our events.

For us, they are often hand-delivered by their fundraiser and provide a great follow up conversation opportunity. I can't tell you how many donors have contacted us to have reprints for their family made.

This new medium is a fantastic way to honor and recognize without the "item" stigma. We build this recognition piece into all of our planning and one of our staff members begins the work even before the event, building the shell and text, then popping in the photos afterwards.

If you have student workers or interns in your office, this is a great job for them. They love being involved in the creative process.

THE NESTEGG OF MR. X

DONOR RELATIONS
AND FOLLOW-THROUGH

Lately I have been thinking a great deal about what donor relations means to our organizations, and how we as professionals can better express that to both our internal constituents and our donors as well. Boiling down our profession into an elevator speech isn't easy, so I wanted to discuss one of the traits of a finely honed donor relations shop: follow-through.

At the core of what we do is building and enhancing relationships. But what does that look like? For me, a big part of it is doing what I said I was going to, never letting a ball drop or a donor slip through the cracks, taking the extra step to make sure the circle is complete.

You might be saying, "This seems pretty basic, Lynne, duh!"

It might seem that way, so let me share an anecdote that happened to me. Mr. X received a letter from his scholarship student and, in turn, sent a letter to my VP asking for some more detailed information on the student and his fund. This, in turn, was handed over to me. I pulled all of the information together, read the student letter – a great one! – and worked on a response to the donor. Since good donor relations is in the details, I also noticed that the letter came in an envelope from another university upstate. I mentioned it in my letter and off it went to Mr. X.

Four days later, I received another letter from Mr. X thanking me for my prompt response and a check for $4,000; my favorite kind of letters. After looking up his giving history, we noticed that he gave $1,000 faithfully to his scholarship every year, never more, never less. After giving a copy of the letter and gift to my VP, we decided that he should call Mr. X to thank him personally for his increase.

I sat in our VP's office anxiously as he called Mr. X in his office at said upstate school. He was so gracious and warm; he hadn't had a call from a fundraiser here in a while because we believed he had made his last gift. In fact, this wasn't the case. Mr. X asked VP if he could come down for a visit and for Shabbat. He wanted to meet his student. No problem. And then the other shoe dropped, "Can I also talk to you about leaving my estate to you?" He had no children, was a professor, was about to retire, and had quite a nestegg!

You see, he had requested information from other places he donated by writing their VPs and we were the only ones to respond personally and with detailed enthusiasm. We made a difference simply through good donor relations and proper follow-through. To be honest, a $1,000 a year donor isn't noteworthy for us. But *every* donor deserves the type of follow through he received.

And that is good donor relations. It is also good for your metrics. Talk about tangible outcome of a stewardship effort! I can track every penny of that bequest and $4,000 to our direct efforts; that isn't subjective.

So when you are evaluating and measuring the effectiveness of your program, is follow-through one of your metrics?

PLAQUE: NOT JUST A DENTAL ISSUE!

RETHINKING YOUR RECOGNITION

We seem, as an industry, to have plaque disease.

When I was at Rollins College, one of the activities I undertook, with the help of my two work study students, was to photograph and catalog in a searchable database every named space and plaque on campus. It took us an entire summer, but was really worth it! We even transcribed the writing in case the plaque was lost. If I tried that at other schools, I would need a small army and a decade.

You see, the thing about plaques is that they are often problematic. We seem to be obsessed with them, though. How many of us have had nightmare stories where the plaque has been misspelled, or the portrait looked like a bad jailhouse tattoo. I'm the girl that, when I visit any museum, hospital, university, I'm always looking at the plaques and walls to see if they're as bad as mine!

All of my vendor friends at companies that make plaques are going to groan over this, but other than for naming recognition, what purpose do plaques serve? Should we be guiding our donors and fundraisers into a different form of recognition and stewardship?

Playing devil's advocate, there exists the argument that plaques serve as a lasting legacy for the donor and institution. Agreed, but is there a better way? I can't tell you how many plaques I have seen "lost" or "misplaced" when renovations or office moves happen. There has to be a better way than trusting these expensive bronze weighty monuments to "Fred" from facilities.

Now, I'm not saying get rid of them altogether. What I am asking for is that we, as professionals, encourage those we work with to find mediums in which to recognize and tell stories other than mounted brass.

Is it time for a deep cleaning? Sorry, bad pun, but I couldn't help myself!

DIGITAL DONOR RECOGNITION

ADDING FUTURE FLEXIBILITY

Recently, I installed my very first digital donor recognition piece. It was a fascinating process and a whirlwind of donor relations fun. Here are the things I learned along the way!

It all began with the fundraiser and the director of alumni relations coming to me and saying they needed a plaque. This project focused around the University's basketball team, and telling the history of the team, listing the past captains, and also expressing the impact that a coach has had on the program, all very difficult to do in a traditional plaque format. Well, as I just mentioned in the previous chapter, since I have a firm aversion to plaques, I called a meeting to investigate.

As we sat across a conference room table, I asked a couple of key questions:

1. Who's paying? Turns out a donor set aside $25k of their gift for this purpose.

2. Where us it going to go? The gym.

3. Has anyone told athletics? Blank stares.

4. How is a listing on a plaque going to tell a story? Blank states again.

5. What if a captain we didn't know about surfaces? Well you get my drift...

So, brilliant mind that I am – and I mean that in a sarcastic manner – I said, "What about a digital recognition display?"

Blank stares.

Then, "What would that do?" Aha! Lightbulb moment! It can play videos, tell stories, have text, audio, listing of captains, message from the President, photos, history of the program, and even donor recognition for those who contribute to the scholarship fund in honor of the coach! As I see the eyes light up across the room and the wheels begin to spin, I realize I might have gotten in over my head. How much will this cost? I had no clue.

So a plan was set forth: fundraiser would obtain donors, I would get three quotes from vendors, and alumni would start gathering ideas. One minor thing; we had never done anything remotely digital, and boy do we love our Brass plaques. It would be a dynamic change and perhaps would take some convincing. After receiving three bids from vendors I met through ADRP, we had another meeting, this time with athletics at the table. The range of bids was astounding and we began to narrow the field based on functionality, deadline, customer service, and price.

In addition to our digital piece, we worked with our communications department to design a colorful background with images that corresponded. Then we sought approval from the funding donor who loved the idea! After an approval if our VP, the process began in earnest. (It is important to note here that each person on the team had an assigned role, from content, to event for the revealing, etc.)

I served as overall project manager and found it to be a thought-provoking and challenging exercise coordinating everyone from facilities, IT, vendors, communications, athletics, and others as needed.

The great thing about digital recognition is that it can be changed at any time; if there is a mistake, an omission, more robust content and greater lists of donors, it can all be changed easily. Once the background arrived, it was mounted and the next day the piece was mounted and tested. After many nervous moments it came to life!

SO. MANY.
HORS D'OEUVRES.

ARE YOUR EVENTS REALLY
DONOR-CENTERED?

No matter where I go, I end up saying similar things to folks who ask me about which event is best to recognize and engage their donors: events aren't a silver bullet to donor recognition and engagement.

Allow me to take that one step further by saying that a vast majority of the events that donors are invited to are *not* donor centered. By their very nature, you are asking a donor to do something that they may or may not want to participate in. You tell them the following:

- You need to show up on *this* date

- You need to show up at *this* time

- You need to eat and drink *this* that *we* picked

- You'll sit next to the people *we* choose for you (good grief)

- You'll hear about things *we* want to tell you (sometimes for a looooong time)

199

- You'll have to get gussied up no matter how long your day in the office

- You *can't* bring your kids (or maybe you shouldn't)

So my question to you is: why should I go? And what happens if, God forbid, I already have plans that evening? If I miss the event, do I miss the whole experience?

These type of traditional donor events are *organization* centered, not *donor* centered.

So what gives? Why do we keep doing it the same all the time?

The answer: Because I guess no one challenged the status quo: "We've always done it that way."

Events are a time where a donor should be immersed in the special experiences that only your organization can offer. They should be fully sensory and interactive, and they shouldn't make the donor feel bad for not wanting to hear from every single member of your leadership in 3-5 minute stints.

So how do we fix this?

We start designing events donors want to come to, and we start doing events that are smaller and more customized. In addition, for those who can't attend, we don't ignore them.

Okay, so what does that event look like? I have a rule about events – and excuse the candor here folks – it should be an event I want to get off of my couch for and put on my bra. You're laughing, but I'm serious.

Why do I want to come and eat your baked chicken? What is it that I will experience that I can't unless I go? I say it all the time, but there's only so many heavy hors d'oeuvres a person can eat in a lifetime, believe me. Why should I be herded together with hundreds of other semi-wealthy to wealthy people and given the same speech? Where am I in all of this? Or is this really about *you*?

Sometimes, it's going to be about *us*, like campaign launches and when I get to meet the beneficiary of my giving, but most of the time, it's really about *you*. And frankly, I grow tired of that. What is a unique experience that I can touch, taste, see, smell, interact with that only you can provide? Once you've seen a ballroom and hotel carpet, you've kind of seen them all. What sets yours apart?

One outstanding example is the University of Central Florida athletics department. They had their top loyal supporters come in and experience what it was like to go through an official recruiting visit; that's TOP NOTCH, folks. Imagine how exciting for the donors that must have been to get that kind of special treatment and behind-the-scenes access!

So my challenge to you is to make one or two changes that turn your events into something that your donors thrill and delight at attending.

Remember, it's not about *you*, it's about the *donor*.

DIPPING SAUCE ON MY NEW VERSACE

TIPS FOR DONOR EVENTS

I thought it was about time to write something on events. Some of you do events as a part of your daily duties, while others of you volunteer or attend or give feedback. Below are my tips and tricks, some tried and true, while some may be new to you and some may confirm your philosophies.

THERE IS NO EXCUSE FOR A HANDWRITTEN NAME TAG. EVER.

There are Dymo name tag printers, Brother label makers, and portable wireless printers. Simple, cheap, effective ways for you never to use a Sharpie for name tags again.

DON'T DRINK ON THE JOB

I have *never* had a drop of alcohol at an event I was working or volunteering. Don't get me wrong, I've had plenty after, but never during. And, for that matter, I usually never eat unless seated with guests. That's what tastings are for. If a crisis or medical event were to occur, I want a clear head and the ability to transport someone and meet their needs should something happen. If you need to appear like you are drinking, have a tonic or ginger ale with lime. Seriously, not worth it.

NEGOTIATE AN EXTRA ROOM

Whenever I am doing a seated dinner, I *always* negotiate a complimentary private room from the hotel or space. If something happens, you will need somewhere private to be able to take a guest so they aren't publicly embarrassed. For example, consider the elderly or those who have overindulged. Having thought ahead about a place for them to rest is priceless.

BEING PREPARED IS NECESSARY

I always have the following with me: sewing kit, safety and bobby pins, Shout wipes or Tide pen, first aid kit, hairspray, cuff links, and pony tail holders. Believe me, I have rescued many a million dollar donors' evenings with one of those items and amazed them in the process.

ALWAYS DO A FOOD TASTING

I spend good money on food, sometimes sacrificing flowers or other items, because the food is memorable, especially in certain crowds. When you plan the food, you should always have a tasting; any caterer that won't let you isn't a good caterer. Take it from a former pastry chef here, it matters.

Here's why: It may sound delicious and the photos of it may be grand, but what is the actual eating process going to look like for your guests? Will it be awkward? Will the dipping sauce drip on my new Versace? (I *hate* dipping sauces at events; they're landmines.) I don't know any society lady that wants spinach or poppy seeds in her expensive veneers...I could do a whole write up on food.

IF YOU ARE RESPONSIBLE FOR THE ENTIRE EVENT, DON'T WORK REGISTRATION

Staff your event wisely, have someone with a *meh* personality? Don't have them serve as a greeter. Put them somewhere useful, but don't let them be the first or last impression of your event. When staffing your event, make sure to communicate your expectations to your volunteers and follow through.

INVEST IN SOME COMMUNICATION DEVICES

Buy good walkie-talkies/radios with the neat secret service headsets. You won't regret it. Don't forget to give one to the venue and the caterer for clear communication, then train your volunteers to find someone with a radio for questions or situations. This is amazingly helpful, and discreet...even in small venues. Bonus, you get to look like a spy talking into your lapel or wrist. You can co-purchase with the team that does commencement and share; they will really appreciate it!

PREPARE A TRAY FOR YOUR HOST

For your president, CEO, host, whoever is your key person, have a tray made with dinner and some fresh fruit to go. Most of them don't eat as they are busy with the schmooze and presentation and will really appreciate your thoughtfulness.

DON'T LET YOUR DECOR GO TO WASTE

We spend good money on flowers. I order a bunch of poly-vinyl vases (at a dollar each) and have the florist arrange them so, at the end of the night, I can treat some of the ladies to beautiful take home flowers! MUCH better than a silly tchotchke.

If you have to do a giveaway – I am strongly opposed – think edible, like a chocolate die cast of your logo or symbol. Or you can do what I do now, take half of your budget for gifts and give it to your general scholarship fund. How will you let donors know? The next year you can have the student who received the money from your event speak, a donor relations full circle moment. And your attendees will love it!

BE MORE EFFICIENT WITH PROGRAMS

Stop wasting money on printed programs, menu cards, scrolls of honor, and table place cards invest in technology to wow your attendees. I invested in digital photo frames with my logo and place two on each table or on cocktail tables with the slide show of program, menu, and notes about forgoing the giveaway, etc. Now, I would purchase tablets on sale or use iPads as you can reuse them over and over and, at the end of the night, aren't throwing away money on printing. And it is so green! Take it a step further and buy individual gobos with company logos to project onto their tables so they know where to sit, you can even project individual names on to tables to prevent those pesky name card swappers; hard to move yourself if your name is projected on a table... Muahaha!

SOAKING UP THE SUN

SUMMER PROJECT IDEAS

Just like spring cleaning at home, summer projects are a ritual in development offices across the land. Once the fog clears from commencement, parking spaces and elevator room opens up, the cafeteria offerings begin to look noticeably lighter, and vacations begin to empty the offices nearby.

Summer is a great time to work on your program and help solve some of the issues that caused you to have heartburn, a large Starbucks tab (or other vices) over the last year. Below are some of my ideas.

STREAMLINE YOUR PROCESSES

Is your acknowledgment process slow and clunky? Is it time to breathe new life into it with new letters? Look into how to streamline the process and find letters shared from colleagues.

SEND OUT SURVEYS

Do your endowment reports suck the life out of you? Can you find a better way to pull together the data needed or to get students to cooperate? Are they pleasing your donors? Don't know? You may want to implement a survey or feedback mechanism so that you can find out if your work is fruitful and satisfies your target audience.

IMPLEMENT NEW IDEAS

Did you recently attend a conference and come back inspired? Want to implement a new idea you've seen elsewhere, or something that could increase your donor satisfaction and visibility? Now is the time.

GET A FEW QUICK WINS TO INCREASE THE DONOR FOCUS SIDE OF YOUR SHOP

- Work with your gift processing team to have the Donor Bill of Rights placed on every gift receipt.

- Work with your online giving team to make the online thank you and acknowledgment more donor friendly.

- Post the Donor Bill of Rights on your webpage.

These three quick changes can show your donors your intent and make others more aware of their needs.

BUILD A MISSION, VISION, AND TASK/WORK CALENDAR FOR YOUR OFFICE

Let others know your beliefs, and also show them the projects you are working on so they can help understand your workload. Also, write down a list of all of the things that derailed your plans or otherwise interrupted your year. Analyze them and try to learn how to head them off at the pass to make your future smoother.

ANALYZE YOUR BUDGET

Look at places you overspent, look for hidden reserves, and make sure your projects were worthwhile, both in donor focus and also fiscally.

If you have budget reserves and need to spend them before the end of the fiscal year, here are some great ideas: high quality color laser printer, nametag printers (Dymo are best), professional development, consultant fees, digital video camera, or organizational supplies.

CALL UP YOUR VENDORS

They will give you ideas for the next big thing, send you samples and new catalogs for the new year, and also let you know if any of your favorites are on sale. They are a great resource for trend information and what's working right now.

CALL A FEW COLLEAGUES IN YOUR INDUSTRY

Bench marking and sharing ideas is so valuable. You can commiserate, brainstorm, and talk to others who do what you do. Never forget the value your professional network.

TALK TO YOUR STAFF

That is, if you have one – or else talk yourself, but be careful and do it with the door closed. Also talk to key stakeholders to find out if they have any new creative ideas that can help your program or your donors. Try to implement at least one of those ideas in the coming year.

WRITE THANK YOU NOTES TO THOSE WHO HAVE HELPED YOU SUCCEED IN THE PAST YEAR

This means facilities staff, data folks, mail room personnel, all of the people who have gotten you out of a pinch or whose work makes your life easier. They will be surprised and delighted.

STOP, TAKE A DEEP BREATH, AND BE APPRECIATIVE

Appreciate the wonderful careers we have ensuring that the many missions of our organizations help the world be a better place. And if you have trouble doing that, you can always work on your resume.

PART 4

UNIQUE DONOR POPULATIONS

THE STEWARDSHIP BUS DRIVER

LET DATA DRIVE YOUR STRATEGY

One can give many answers when someone asks, "Where do I start?" For me, the beginning always lies in the data, something that I think, for many people, is an afterthought, a measure of ROI instead of the driving factor for their strategy.

Data should be at the beginning and at the core of everything we do. I often ask people about their data, tell me how many reports they send, how many letters they write, how many scholarship funds do they steward. Usually, these answers for most professionals are burned into their memories.

But if I dig even below the surface, the ground becomes much muddier. How many consecutive donors of ten or more years do you have? How many donors are in your giving societies? What is your current retention rate from year 1 to 2, year 2 to 3? I am often met with blank stares and replies of, "Should I know that?" If you don't know some basic numbers and analyze what they mean for you and your program, how can you build an effective strategy?

So here are a short list of reports you can have pulled so you can analyze the data and determine how it affects your strategy, or have you even considered some of these items? I recommend all of these reports be pulled looking at the last 5 years.

1. Pull a giving pyramid report: How many donors at each level do you have? Does yours look like a pyramid, a sombrero, an hourglass, or a space needle? There are strategies for each shape, just like clothing... Ha ha!

2. How many donors do you have giving consecutively for 5, 10, 15, 20 or more years? These are great people who are under-stewarded and make wonderful planned giving prospects. A note here for your data team: pull by calendar year, not fiscal. Most of these donors don't know or care about our calendars.

3. How many first time donors did you have last year? What did you do for them?

4. What is your retention rate from year 1 to 2? 2 to 3? Where is your drop off? How do you help?

5. Break out your donors by the method in which they give? How many give online, direct mail, phonathon? Then target your stewardship in their preferred medium of communication.

6. For those of you in higher education, there are three essential reports:

   a. Pull a list of your married alumni. Sounds simple, but have you done it?

   b. Pull a list of folks that have earned more than one degree from your institution.

   c. Pull a list of those who have undergraduate degrees vs graduate degrees with their giving histories. This one will astonish you!

7. Find out how many people with email addresses you have, a raw percentage. If it is under 50%, you have work to do; over 75%, you're my hero.

8. Event attendance: people who attend events are engaged and more likely to give! Who are these folks? Are our events strategic? Or are we just getting the same folks over and over? There are some people that will attend the opening if a door if there's free food.

So about now your brains are churning and you're forwarding this to your data team in a curtly worded email along the lines of, "How come we don't do this?" or "I need all of these by end of business today!"

STOP!

Our data folks are our friends, and just like the facilities staff, are our secret weapons for success! Meet with them, bake them brownies (techies love sugar), take them to lunch, and *then* show them this post. Most will get really excited, some will give an audible sigh, and some will even knock your socks off by saying, "I have all of those, I was waiting for someone to ask me for them!" You will be a genius!

So firm a partnership and work through these reports with them, forming bonds over gaps in the data, they will tell you how you can help them, you'll learn a great deal, and it will be a win win proposition. And if you hear the fateful words, "it's not possible!" call or email me and we can work on making forward progress for you together. Better yet, have your data folks call me!

Once you have all of this data gold mining done, it is up to *you* to analyze it, build strategies and partnerships, and learn how to change those numbers more positive in the future.

OVER-INVOLVED DONORS

HAVING THE CRUCIAL CONVERSATION

Seems like an oxymoron doesn't it? Our whole profession is built on the premise that we do as much as possible to engage our constituents and have them move closer to our organization. But when is close too close? Recent events in the news remind us that, while donors are partners in our organizations and trusted friends and allies in the good fight, there is a professional distance that needs to be demonstrated.

For those of us in universities, this is demonstrated mostly in donors wanting to establish a scholarship, and then have control over the recipients or the selection process. This is a big no-no. Donors cannot be involved in the selection of students and cannot make the qualifications so restrictive that the scholarship can only be given to one student. This isn't a gift; it's a tuition payment and isn't tax deductible. If you have a situation like this, work to remedy it immediately. It's not beneficial for you or your organization and can lead to disastrous results.

This may require you to have some "crucial conversations" with colleagues, leadership, and even donors. Don't know what a "crucial conversation" is? I highly suggest everyone in the non-profit world buy the book *Crucial Conversations*, read it and then share it. I promise, I don't get a percentage of the sales, but if this book can help you the way it has helped me, that's all the benefit I need.

As donors and our relationships with them become more complex and their needs become more sophisticated, it is indeed our pleasure and our burden to help manage these expectations and desires with the realities, legalities, and organizational priorities. At its essence, it becomes an educational process for our constituents, our staff, and ourselves.

What does this process look like? I would highly recommend you use the Donor Bill of Rights and the statement of ethical guidelines as a beginning for your efforts and move forward from there. The great thing about these documents is that they set up a wonderful framework that can serve as a guide for your efforts. I would also say that there are elements of gut instincts and common sense that come into play here. The old adage about things too good to be true usually applies. More interestingly, this educational process will allow our organizations to enhance communications and break down silos to further productive effort that funnel back to the mission of our organizations.

At the core of what we do is engagement and relationship building. But like all relationships, boundaries must be established and built so that there are productive results for all involved. Donors don't want to be caught up in the fallout from a mess and organizations cannot afford to lose the trust of their other donors by suffering the consequences of a relationship gone wrong. Learn from others' mistakes and make sure that you, as the donor's advocate and engagement officer keep these things in mind as relationships are built.

MID-LEVEL DONORS

LOOKING BEYOND THE DATA

As I travel across the country as a speaker and consultant, helping people assess their stewardship programs and build a mid-level giving strategy, I often ask for a pile of data ahead of my visit. Inevitably in the package from every organization I visit, large and small, are the ubiquitous LYBUNT and SYBUNT reports. These reports are often the bedrock of an organization's data mining and data collection, and every time I see them I smirk and shake my head.

When I finally arrive on site, one of the first questions I ask is, "What do these reports tell us about our constituencies?" I often get blank stares and then inevitably someone attempts to tell me and define LYBUNT or SYBUNT. I know what they are, and I know why these reports were once deemed important and useful, but what these reports fail to allow us to see is any connection or depth about the constituent except for their ability to write a check or enter credit card numbers.

We have to stop thinking about our donors transactionally and start thinking of them as round, dynamic, and diverse populations of people who are engaged with our organizations. This is especially true for the mid-level donors. We know they give solidly year after year at more than a token level, and we know they haven't yet made their first major gift, but what else do we know?

Because our staff is often focused at the top or bottom of the giving pyramid, these loyal and engaged donors are often left in the gap. In addition, how many organizations have stewardship plans, cultivation strategies, and solicitation staff dedicate to this group? I would argue, not many.

But before we build plans, strategies, and invest human resources, we must learn more about them. Do they attend our events, open our emails, or engage with us on social media? How do they identify themselves and their affiliation with our organizations? And, how do we find out this information?

These mid-level donors will help us build our strategy if we engage them in meaningful ways and compile data that is more robust and deep than just giving history and wealth. We give the donors the opportunity to engage, interact, and make choices. Then we analyze those who are most identified by the traits of a mid-level donor — loyalty, engagement, interaction, targeted meaningful philanthropy — and *then* we implement based on their needs. This is much like we already do with our major donors, and look at the success! After all, these are major donors in training, no?

What are the rewards? Our ROI increases exponentially as these are fiercely loyal donors, once treated properly, and we build a cadre of constituent profiles that are rich, deep, and fruitful. So the next time you think about your mid-level donors, I hope that you will see them in a different lens than before.

CONSECUTIVE/LOYALTY DONORS

WHAT ARE YOU DOING FOR THEM?

I am a proud supporter of my alma mater, The University of South Carolina (*Go Gamecocks!*). And every year, I make my annual gift. After I make my gift, I receive the usual receipt and acknowledgment, but I also receive something special, I am a member of the Carolina Circle, something USC reminds me of every year. I receive a postcard and the back of it is a vinyl decal, which is proudly displayed on my back window along with my Gamecock Club membership decal, a constant reminder of their acknowledgment of my consistent giving.

The Carolina Circle is for those of us who have given consistently, at any amount, for the past three years or more. This simple gesture enhances in me the feeling that USC values me and knows that my gift matters, its just good donor relations. And so that leads me to ask you, what are you doing for your consecutive donors? Do you know who the are? How many you have? What do they "look" like? If you haven't thought about these folks, I challenge you to take a new look. Every time I visit with one of my consulting clients during their donor relations audits, this is one of my consistent areas of focus.

Here are some reasons for focus you might not be aware of:

1. Consistent donors are the *best* planned giving prospects. Period.

2. Consistent donors are usually present at many of your events, and make sure to support you in their community.

3. Consistent donors make *great* volunteers, spokespeople and helpers.

4. They are deeply committed to your cause and I would argue that telling their stories is *more* valuable than your "major donors."

5. Consistent donors make *great* focus groups and survey folks. They have been around for a while and can tell you what has worked and where you can improve.

6. The ROI on these efforts is *huge*. Remember, it's 7 times cheaper to keep the donors you have happy than to go out and acquire new ones!

So now we go back to the central question: what have you done for them lately? If you hesitate or have no idea, this might be a good time to start recognizing them. You don't have to create a society or a big to do around them, but you should recognize their importance and build this group into your strategic donor relations planning.

A few simple ideas:

1. A postcard like USC's, with or without a decal or magnet.

2. A special email or video for them. A communication that lets them know they are valued and you know who they are and why they matter.

3. Invite them to the same events your major donors are invited to. Remember, it's the thought of inclusion that matters for them.

4. Feature them and tell their stories in your publications, have one of them speak at your next event, etc. A lifetime of good will is headed your way, and other donors will identify with them more than they can the mega million trustee type donor.

5. Run a thank-a-thon just for them. Have staff, volunteers, students, anyone call them to thank them, and JUST thank them, for their loyal support and devotion to your mission!

NOTICE: I didn't say mail them a random tchotchke or have an event just for them. That's not the idea here folks. If you need to clean out your closets, do it some other way. If you want another event to plan, find a different strategy: honest tough love.

CHAMPIONS, FRIENDS, ACQUAINTANCES

DO YOU KNOW WHAT IS MEANINGFUL?

I am always reading the newest and latest survey of donor motivations, online giving, and other factors about donors. Recently, my friend Ann sent me a new report and white paper based on a new segmentation entitled, "Champions, friends, and acquaintances"; you can find the entire report online. But for those of you without long subway commutes (I highly frown upon reading charts and graphs while driving) I thought I would give you some key point and my thoughts on them here.

This study truly reinforces a multi-channel approach to donor communications that I have been advocating for years now. What is most notable here is the donor's strong preference for email. This preference encompasses an ever increasing shift in constituent mindset. While personal communication for many of us is king, what we realize here is that our donors rely on email not only for its convenience, but also for its perceived cost savings to an organization where fiscal responsibility is paramount.

However, before we dismiss print and face-to-face meetings altogether, we must realize that, once again, data must drive our strategy. If we do not possess the email addresses for our champions, how can we effectively communicate in their preferred manor?

This leads me to advocate to all of you the importance of email acquisition in every part of your donor interactions. But how can we obtain email addresses? Here are a few tips:

- In order to attend an event, they must give you an email address. Period. That means guests, alumni, friends, anyone who gets a free cocktail and passed snack, gives an email address. When they register or RSVP, if you don't have their email, ask for it or have an iPad out with an easy email form to input data as they come in the door.

- Go to your fundraisers and empty their Outlook contacts and input them in your database; you'd be surprised what you will find.

- Run an in house email acquisition campaign. That means faculty, administration, and staff, anyone who has contact, pull those emails out and place them in your database.

- Finally, you can run an email acquisition campaign through social media and to help find lost alumni and friends.

One of the best takeaways from this new segmentation of constituents prompted me to think about my friends and acquaintances and what I can do to bring them to champions.

As many of you know, I am a big believer in the bless and release philosophy. The fact remains that for all of the good work we do and the effort and dollars spent, some of our acquaintances will never become friends or champions. Bless them and then release them. Focus your efforts on moving those friends to champions. When you have perfected that and have tons of hours on your hands, and have exhausted your online shopping budget, you can focus on the disengaged.

When you get there, call me, I want to know what that feels like.

How exactly do we do this? Here are some tips:

- We must find out from them, through feedback methods and analytics, what it is that is meaningful to them. From the three case studies in the white paper, we can see that depending on the organization, these populations can differ, yet some of their behavioral tendencies are mirrored. We must segment and adapt our messaging, sometimes by repurposing the same message and targeting each group intentionally, and then analyzing their engagement, response, and interest.

- Once we have tendencies and donor motivations for each group, we can better communicate with our friends and acquaintances and ask them what would it take to move them into the champion group.

- Additionally, learning from our donors what other organizations they support and benchmarking with those other organizations and learning from them is vital. We all have a great deal to learn from not only our donors (if we ask them) but also from each other. See something constantly cross your desk from a board member or champion that is produced by another organization? Pick up the phone and call them, learn about their methodologies and how they view their segments of constituents. You'll accomplish a couple of important things.

  1. You'll make the day of the person you call to flatter.

  2. You'll come away with new ideas for your program and you'll be able to tell your donor about the experience and build a stronger bridge to them by demonstrating you can listen and that their feedback is meaningful to them.

THE GREY AREAS

THE HIGH-NEEDS DONOR

As we enter a new era of philanthropy in the 21st century, particularly in post-recession times, donors' giving habits and expectations are changing dramatically. They often expect greater levels of transparency and accountability, which is a boon for donor relations professionals as we help to educate fundraisers and other administrators of the importance of stewardship.

However, this assertiveness by donors crosses into many grey areas. The place where this tendency is most evident is that of scholarships. Weekly, donor relations professionals on countless discussion boards, listservs, and emails face the tried, true, and tricky question: "Donor A wants to select or help select their scholarship student. Is this okay?" My answer is always a resounding "NO" citing IRS regulations that then this is no longer a gift anymore.

Despite all advice about how to handle a conversation like this with a donor, I know it is difficult. Having had a great deal of exposure to "high-needs" donors over time has taught me that once properly explained, most philanthropists understand, at least after the 2nd or 3rd try. A donor can always put criteria restrictions in the gift agreement. However, the most savvy fundraisers know that the more restrictions, the less likely the fund is able to easily be distributed. This applies not only to scholarships and chairs but also to things like research funds, and directed use funds. I believe that this is where good relationship building and donor relations is most key, allowing donors and fundraisers the room to have the "Crucial Conversations" necessary to make both sides happy and feel good about the gift.

TOLERATING THE PUPPY STAGE

WELCOMING BACK LAPSED DONORS

As we think about proactive and strategic donor relations and how we move the needle on ever-falling donor retention rates, I am constantly thinking of new ways to reinforce and encourage good donor behavior.

My colleague recently got a five month old puppy, his first indoor dog. I was giving him some tips for training and tolerating the puppy stage and for reinforcing good behavior, and in my mind it reminded me a great deal of donor relations. In building donor retention, one of the things we want to do is encourage the donor behavior we desire from our donors.

How do we do this? A few methods are proving to be most effective: first time donor welcome programs, consecutive donor recognition, and other programs can be wonderful for reinforcement as well.

But what happens when your lapsed donors – those squirrelly SYBUNTS as we call them – or lapsed or long-lapsed donors give again? Do you have a proactive touch in place to reward them for coming *back*? Have you and your annual giving folks thought or talked about this?

Well my clients and I are thinking about it. Think about how wonderful it is to say to a donor, "You did something great and we noticed!"

It doesn't have to be a postcard or mailing, it doesn't have to be fancy. What if it were an email?

The way we welcome them back can be subtle or overt, but it needs to be done. We need our donors to know that we noticed their behavior and that they are wanted by our organization, not just another number, another check to cash. If we stick with it, and track retention on those lapsed donors, we can build an effective program so they don't leave us again.

Another idea is to reach out to donors who have lapsed and find out why they might have not given again. The best research is from those who have had a donor experience. If we don't know why they left, we can't venture to have them stay with us in the future. Remember that we also need to look at extenuating factors. Donors who pass away lapse; don't let them ruin your numbers.

Also, take the time to examine your "in honor, in memory" donors. Are they likely to stay? Keep their retention separately from your mainstream donors. Yes, I understand this is more work, but it is worthy work to truly understand our donors, their behavior, and their motivations.

THE BIRTHDAY CARD ALTERNATIVE

PLANNED GIVING STEWARDSHIP

What are you doing for your donors who have left their ultimate gift? Several years ago, I spoke at the an organization about incorporating technology into planned giving stewardship with many raised eyebrows. So here are some things to think about.

RETIREMENT RESOURCES

Some places send birthday cards. While these are cute and thoughtful, my Dad for one doesn't want too many reminders that his age creeps up year after year, (he now counts backwards). How about sending strategic information about best using retirement resources? You can send this cheaply by sending a postcard with a link or an email.

WEBCAMS

Yes, most planned giving donors have a computer and internet, they are the #1 growing demographic on Facebook, too, a great way for them to connect with lost classmates! How about sending them webcams or having students and staff teaching them how to Skype with loved ones near and far? My parents love to Skype with me, we had a virtual Christmas this year and I got to see them open their presents live; it was fabulous! Once they have the technology and know how to use it, instead of inviting them to events, have the events come to them incorporating video chats with students, attending classes by webinar, having investment forums where they can learn from you. All of these things steward donors who are otherwise forgotten.

INVITAITON LISTS

Are they on all of your invitation lists? They should be, even if they can't attend, the invitation and inclusiveness is meaningful. Many planned giving donors have vast life experience and would love to share that with your organization; engage them as targeted volunteers. If they are close by, have them guest lecture. Use them to tell their stories in your magazines! My alma mater USC (*Go Gamecocks!*) recently had us write congratulatory notes to recently admitted students – great stewardship of me as a volunteer and a wonderful activity for a planned giving donor to share their experiences!

The idea here is that they not be dismissed and not engaged as a part of your donor community. These are people that have made a wonderful and lasting commitment to your organization and deserve to be celebrated. Even if you do one new thing for them, it's better than what it was!

CORPS AND FOUNDS

CORPORATE AND FOUNDATION STEWARDSHIP

How do I better steward corporations and foundations? The basic premise to my corps and founds philosophy is a simple one: the same way you steward individual donors, just in an enhanced manner.

I started my development career as a grant writer, writing things in 90 pages or less, in triplicate (I jest), and for faceless boards who would decide large grants. The thing is, corps and founds are not nameless faceless entities. A corporation or foundation is made up of people. Plain and simple. We steward gifts made by individuals.

We can steward corps and founds in much the same way. Here are some examples.

ALWAYS WRITE ACKNOWLEDGMENTS

not only the grant maker, but also hand-written notes to your contact at the corp – go a long way as well. It's a relationship, just like any other that needs to be nurtured.

You need not reinvent the wheel here. Many of the programs you have in place for individuals will work well for corps and founds with minor tweaks.

INVITE CORPS AND FOUNDS INTO YOUR GIVING SOCIETIES, ESPECIALLY CUMULATIVE ONES

We did this with the Chevalier society at NYU Poly and the folks just loved attending events and being around our high net worth individuals. I received so many expressions of gratitude for not making them buy a table, which builds loyalty and appreciation.

OFFER REAL IMPACT OF THEIR GIVING

not just in the required grant reporting and annual reports, but in real life. Have them meet students that benefit from their support, have lunch with faculty that are leaders in their field, etc.

PROVIDE UNIQUE ACCESS OPPORTUNITIES

Corporations are always looking for unique event space at low costs, and your organizations and campuses are full of them. Make sure that either your office or the events office is connected to their office of events and planning; it will be an invaluable relationship and mutually beneficial.

Offer your leaders or faculty as facilitators or speakers for their retreats or meetings. This is expertise they would otherwise have to pay top dollar for and they will be most grateful of your thoughtfulness.

HAVE A SIT DOWN CHAT

Especially if you are new, talk about the ways and names of those who should be recognized and how they would best like the recognition. Perhaps you have been sending invitations to people who no longer work there or have been ignoring their branding. This is a place where attention to detail is paramount and can build strong bridges to the future.

EMBRACE INNOVATION

Corporations embrace innovation and technology in far more rapid and encompassing way than we do. Emails, smart phones, and web-based communications are king. Think of digitizing your invites and RSVP process, especially for this population. If you send the CEO paper invites, they will get lost in a stack of thousands. And for that matter, executive assistants rule the earth. Be nice, know that they control your fate, and embrace it.

REMEMBER THE HUMAN ELEMENT

Finally, remember that corps and founds are made up of individual people. As such they have different needs, cultures, personalities and methods. Adapt and change with each one in order to best meet their needs.

THE 110% CLUB

THE NEWEST GROUP OF DONORS

In our daily lives with donors, we have many segments of people to recognize. Those are growing by the minute. How do we reward great donor behavior?

Many of us have built programs that recognize first time donors, loyalty or consecutive donors, mid-level donors, and donors of all shapes and sizes. I am always trying to find new giving patterns and groups to recognize and I think I have stumbled across a new segment needing recognition and encouragement.

Here is your new segment of the future: The 110% club!

Okay, I'm surely not advocating a new giving society or club, as we have plenty of those. But instead, how about we recognize a positive behavior and let the donor know you noticed it?

Here's how it works. Last year Ms. Donor gave you $100, this year when she gave her gift, she gave you $110 or $125, increasing her gift. We want her to know that her increase didn't go unnoticed and we appreciate the extra resources. She has given us 110%. An increase in her gift and a behavior that indicates to us that she is more engaged and we've done something right.

So how do we build this program? What does the recognition look like?

Good question. Here is what I imagine it looking like:

- Have your data folks pull a list of people who increased their gifts by 10-25% last year. We need to know the size of population we're dealing with here. Remember data drives your strategy at all times!

- Then have your data team pull this report weekly for you with current fiscal year donors. This list should be a tickler for you. This tickler should call you to action: can you call these folks, write them a note, or have a volunteer make a special effort to thank them? Don't let these people simply fall through the cracks. If a donor doubles their gift more than once, send someone to visit them pronto.

Remember that some of the main goals of donor relations is to build retention and to encourage good philanthropic behavior in the future, so make sure to recognize that very behavior in sometimes very simple ways.

MOVING THE NEEDLE

FIRST TIME DONOR RETENTION

We talk a great deal about impressions. I often discuss how we are judged, whether we like it or not. I'd like to touch on a specific area of donor relations: first time donors.

I believe it is imperative that you build and implement a first time donor program for your organization. Most organizations have a 20 to 25 percent retention rate for their first time donors. This is simply unacceptable.

My first question for you is: what is your rate? The second is: what are you doing about it? If you moved the needle on first time donor retention by 5 or 10 percent, it would mean a great deal monetarily to your organization. In addition, it is a measurable way to tell if your donor relations program is performing well. If your retention rate is less than 60 percent, you've got work to do. Imagine if you were a restaurant and only 4 out of 10 of your customers left after their first meal. You'd be out of business within months.

So what can we do? The first step is to do something! But here is an example of a first time donor program that, in three years, has raised retention from 48 to 72 percent. This has impacted many dollars and hundreds of donors each year.

1. The first thing is the first time donor postcard; it is sent within 30 days of their first gift. This is in addition

to their regular receipt and acknowledgment based on gift level and giving medium. Here's the great thing: you only have to print or design these things once. After all, there is only one first gift!

2. Within the next quarter or so they receive a phone call thanking them for their gift and specifically recognizing them as a first time donor.

3. Then in the next quarter, they receive a hand-written note from a student through our thank-a-donor-a-week program.

4. Finally, a month before the anniversary of their first gift, they receive a final impact piece telling how we used their money, with a soft ask for this year's gift.

It is all coordinated and it all mentions their first gift being meaningful to us. It is done *regardless* of amount! You could replace any of these with a creative video or touch, maybe a link to resources on your web page. We also feature one or two first time donors a year in publications and online. It is crucial we show that their first gift was meaningful and had an impact on our organization.

Here is what we don't do: send tchotchkes or widow decals, add them to a giving society, ask them again for a gift the month after they give, and other silliness. Many first time donors are just engaging with you and see their gift as sort of a test to see how you will treat them. I once heard from a donor at a conference that when he first started giving, he sent out ten $1,000 checks and didn't give to those anymore that didn't write to him or treat him well. His giving is now in the millions for the organizations that did.

It is true that we want every donor to feel special and wonderful about giving; that's one of the aims of donor relations. But this first time group needs special attention when they give their money and trust us for the first time.

VOLUNTEER RECOGNITION

DONOR RELATIONS' FORLORN STEPCHILD

BY DEBBIE MEYERS

Meet volunteer recognition – the Rodney Dangerfield of our profession, the afterthought of many advancement programs.

Time is every bit as valuable as money. Just ask someone dying how much they'd pay for one more week, one more day. So if time is truly such a precious commodity, why don't we recognize volunteers, who give us their time and talent, as much or as well as we recognize our donors?

Well, for starters, it's not as easy as it sounds to quantify and qualify non-monetary contributions. Say we start with the formula that T2 > \$, where T2 equals time and talent, and \$ equals treasure.

That is, what people do for or on behalf of your institution is just as valuable as their financial support.

But this isn't algebra, it's human beings who are innately difficult to objectively measure. Most software packages have little in the way of tracking volunteer activities, other than simple indications like club or advisory board affiliation, a random contact report or event attendance. How would we enter "She's our best volunteer" into a database?

For argument's sake, say we're in a magical world where we know exactly which volunteers did what, and we came up with some flawless rating scale for quantity and quality of their activities. We wouldn't need to ask questions like, how much effort did they expend? What is the actual value of their efforts? How sincere were they? Did someone twist their arms to help out, or did they step up on their own?

Assume all those answers were condensed, analyzed, and then measured on a scientific scale; just for this exercise, make that a scale of 1-10. We'd be able to run reports that tell us the level of commitment and value of each of our volunteers. We're set to create a first-class recognition program, running it by the numbers.

Even at that, we'd face lots of challenges. We would have to address consistency across your institution. Thanks and recognition should be relative and equitable. A volunteer ranked at, say, a 10 who serves on one advisory board should not be treated to a black tie dinner for his service, yet only get listed in a publication for giving a testimonial speech at an event for another department.

In donor relations, we handle a similar situation through varying levels of perks and recognition through our giving societies. The difference is, we know, with fair certainty – other than counting joint giving or matching gifts – who has given us $100,000 cumulatively. Case closed.

And, we know that most donors want – beyond recognition, thanks and accountability – are access and information. So what does that mean for a volunteer? Perhaps an annual recognition event? A letter from our leader? A window cling?

All that aside, volunteer recognition is simple. It's all a matter of the Golden Rule. Have you ever volunteered? What made you feel special and appreciated? What left an unpleasant taste in your mouth? More often than not, it's not what

244

institution says or does to recognize its volunteers, it's how that institution does it. Here's a personal example.

As a volunteer in one organization for several years, I would receive a "Thanks for all you do" card, which the leader signed, but did not personalize. He also sent some small plastic pin that must have been bought in quantities of 500 or 1,000 as a token of thanks. It wasn't clear that he even know what all I did.

Granted, I'm more sensitive to this type of thing than the average person because saying thank you is what I do for a living. But I found that action not only a waste of time, but downright insulting. Why not take three minutes and write a personal message, or even just my name?! Why not recognize me and my fellow volunteers in our weekly meeting? IT'S FREE! It's public. It's meaningful.

On the other hand, for another organization, once a year I create the printed program for their annual fundraising event. This non-profit organization sent me an orchid, which I'm sure they received as a donation, and a hand-written, personalized note to thank me for my efforts. The orchid is on the table in my kitchen, and it's a constant reminder of how much they appreciate me, and how appreciated I feel.

Just as bad as not thanking a volunteer properly is not using them, or not using them meaningfully. After meeting with the development director of a non-profit organization, I was honored when she asked if I would be willing to serve on their fundraising board. That was three months ago. Haven't heard "boo" from them since. My positive feelings toward that group now have gone from good, to neutral, to negative. And come on, it's not like people readily volunteer to help organizations raise money!

If we all would simply remember how valuable our volunteers are, we'd have no difficulty recognizing them. They need to know that we view them as the lifeblood of our organizations, however you choose to tell them that. As J. Sargent Shriver said:

> Serve your families. Serve your neighbors. Serve your cities. Serve the poor. Join others who serve. Serve, serve, serve! That's the challenge. For in the end, it will be servants who save us all.

IN MEMORIAM AND IN HONOR GIFTS

BEING A RESOURCE
DURING DIFFICULT TIMES

Every now and then, life challenges us in ways unimaginable.

This week, my friend's father passed away and I have been stewarding the family through the process. Was I prepared? Is this something I've ever done before? Nope. Did my skills in donor relations and stewardship come in very handy? Absolutely. As a part of the process, we identified two organizations and funds that would receive gifts in lieu of flowers or memorials. It was a difficult process, but in the end a very rewarding one.

Do you have your ducks in a row for donors or families who choose your non-profit in which to donate? If you don't, I highly encourage you examine your processes.

When a bereaved family member or representative calls, who answers the phone and what is the process? Do you have something in place to make it less awkward and troublesome for them?

What does your notification process look like? Can donors sends cards or notes from you to let the family know? Do you have notecards for families who want to send thank yous to the donors? Instead of just giving them a list of people who have contributed, why not also provide them with some beautiful notecards and a pen to help them complete their notes?

I can tell you from a few days of experience that it's wonderful to have someone take care of the details for you, someone you can call at the non-profit to ask questions and help you through the process. Are your notifications simply a modified receipt or is it truly a sensitive and meaningful touchpoint. Have you made sure that the donors who give in honor or in memory of someone don't receive a phone or mail solicitation the next month or quarter?

Have you spoken with your development officers and front line fundraisers? Let's encourage everyone not to establish restricted or endowed funds in memory of someone unless you know there will be adequate gifts to fulfill the minimum. There is nothing worse than a memorial or honorarium fund that goes unspent or doesn't have enough money in it to award. Explaining that to a family is awkward at best. It's hard to tell a family that many their family member's death or loss won't raise the minimum, but it's better to steer them to unrestricted or scholarship or something and then think of recognition later to avoid those pitfalls. I've seen too many memorial gifts go wrong, it can reopen a horrible wound.

Please don't ask the family or representative to complete lots of paperwork in order to make this happen, especially in the beginning. Unfortunately, death brings a great deal of paperwork with it; I was shocked by it, so adding one more thing is an undue burden to them. Help them and offer to be a resource, but take the bureaucracy out of the process if possible.

Many of these things sound like common sense, but you would be amazed at how many people get it wrong.

PART 5

PROFESSIONAL SKILLS AND MANAGEMENT

MEETINGITIS

CREATING MEANINGFUL MEETINGS

As I sat in my 7th meeting of the day last week, I began to drift away...far, far, away. Then on Friday, my trip to Houston was cancelled due to snow and ice and I had an entire day without a single meeting. It was magical, like finding a $20 bill in my coat pocket!

I have a secret. Okay, it's not a well-kept secret, but here goes. I HATE meetings. Abhor them, can't stand them, yet I spend many of my days in them. And I know you do, too. We have a disease in non-profits about meetings. We have meetings about meetings; we have committees about committees. And do you know what? Sometimes we're really unproductive.

Does your organization have meetingitis?

How can you help solve the problem? Don't get me wrong, I'm far from antisocial; I believe in the value of a *good* meeting every now and then, but if you want to punish me, make me attend a meeting where I already know the conclusion because its predetermined and nothing is going to change as a result. I want to pull my eyelashes out!

I have spent so much time in meetings, I feel guilty taking a break to use the restroom, all the while believing that most of the time, I am wasting my time, or it could better be used elsewhere. Here are a few reasons why I thing we fall prey to meetingitis and what we can do about it.

- Stop accepting one-hour meetings as the norm. Move them to thirty-minute meetings, keep them short and focused.

- Always have an agenda with a list of points necessary to cover and stick to it. My friend Mary Solomons is the queen of keeping us on task and focused and I love it!

- One of my clients calls a meeting with the cabinet or high-level executives "an expensive meeting." He's right. How do we reduce the time or necessity of gathering all of the leaders together?

- Can this be accomplished via email or a short phone call? If so, schedule it! People tend to be less social then and more focused on the decision/task at hand.

- Meetings should always end with a summary of action items and a conclusion to move forward.

- Avoid distractions, cell phones, etc., during meetings and have everyone hyper-focused on the task at hand; a half-hour away from email is a great thing. Place all "devices" in the center of the table; the first one who touches it, has to buy lunch or a round of drinks!

- It may be time to push back. While we all want a seat at the table, especially if there are free gummy worms, we may not need to always be there. The higher up in the organization you go, the more meetings you will be asked to attend. Consider these questions:

  - What is the purpose of the meeting? Is it related to my overall goals?

  - What do you expect from me?

  - How long will it last?

- I may need to leave after my contribution. What time will you be dealing with the topics related to me?

- For which part of the agenda will you need my input?

- Do I really need to be there?

- If you need input from our department, can someone else attend instead of me?

- Are decisions likely to be made that only I can make, or can I delegate or sidestep?

- There are few more thrilling opportunities for a junior teammate than being asked to come to a meeting of higher-ups. Why not delegate and have someone serve as your representative? Go with them the first two times, then quietly disappear and leave them to represent you and your team. It will be a growth point for them, you, and your organization.

- Keep your meetings small and focused. When you see a meeting request with 8-12 people on it, it usually means that the organizer didn't know who they should be talking to.

TICK TOCK

TIME MANAGEMENT

I'm asked about this particular topic a great deal. So here's the story, I used to have a full-time job, go to graduate school full-time, and run the Donor Relations Guru (which wasn't a full-time job, though it might as well have been) all in one day. I'm not asking you to pity or envy me, but because I do so much and always have, people often ask how to manage it all.

So I thought I would share some of my tips with you to help you with prioritization and time management. You could be like me and not sleep a great deal, but I don't recommend it at all. Here's what I do recommend.

WORK IN SHORT, FOCUSED BURSTS

I say that I'm a great multitasker, but in all reality, hyper-focus for a limited amount of time is the best way to go. My blog, for example: I wrote every week on my commute into work, headphones on, and I have a focused amount of time to complete the task.

START WITH THE BAD STUFF FIRST

This reminds me of doing homework; I always started with the things I didn't like first, then went from there. It really helps you prioritize.

USE YOUR EMAIL PROPERLY

People are often pleased with my email response time. It's because my inbox isn't full of thousands of messages. My goal at any one time is to have less than 10 in my inbox. I reply and then file it away; if its in my inbox then it is a reminder to complete a task. Keep a great folder system and stick to it. It works wonders. And for goodness sake, don't print emails. Really? You can store them or use a free Outlook tool like Xobni to help you find emails efficiently.

AVOID UNNECESSARY MEETINGS

This means using your calendar effectively, blocking hours of time for focused work, and times when you're not at your best. For example, I am a morning person (rise and shine at 5:00 AM) so if you want a meeting after 4:00 PM with me, you have to outrank me by two. So that means you have to be the VP or President. Period. I never break this rule and it helps greatly.

Also, for those of you managing a staff, trust and empower your staff to go to meetings that are purely informational. It allows your teammates to grow in their skills and frees up some time.

Do you really need a meeting or will a conversation suffice? In non-profit work we tend to have meetings about meetings, under the guise of being good communicators, in reality we're wasting valuable time. We use instant messenger to communicate across offices and within our team and it helps avoid many, many meetings.

DISCOVER AND KNOW YOUR WEAKNESSES

I'm a great data girl and strategist, I'm pretty darn good at manipulating data and creating charts in Excel, but for the life of me I cannot make it print pretty all on one page with headings and all. So I have my teammate help me with that; for a task that would take me two hours, in ten minutes she's done and making me look good.

EFFECTIVELY ASK FOR HELP

Many people just don't know where to begin when everything seems urgent. This is where your boss will earn their big fancy salary. Ask them to help you prioritize. Don't go to them and say, "My plate is too full." Show them three things and make them rank them in order of priorities. Rinse and repeat this step over and over until they understand that their input is not just valuable, but helps drive your strategy. If they can't or won't do this, put together your résumé – no, just kidding...I think. Instead, use donor surveys and data to build a set of priorities and remember that you can't do everything perfectly all at once. Baby steps here; do one thing really well and then move forward. Don't know where to start? Start with my first book, the *Four Pillars of Donor Relations*.

ASK THE RIGHT QUESTIONS IN ORDER TO MOVE YOUR WORK FORWARD.

Before you ask those questions, do some basic research. Before you hit a listserv with 11 bulleted questions or ask an expert for a strategic plan, do your homework. Google the question. Make sure that your question is concise and focused.

I enjoy receiving questions from around the globe, but especially enjoy those that are specific, targeted, and well focused. The ones I tend to ignore on listservs are those that can be answered with Google and those that have more than 5 questions and could be answered in a day of professional development. Show me you've done your part and I'll bend over backwards to help provide you tools and resources for free.

MARCHING ANTS

MANAGING YOUR WORKLOAD

One of the most difficult challenges we face as fundraising professionals is that of balance, time management, and prioritization. Here is a list of tips and tricks I use to help manage the daily (over) flow of priorities, tasks, and life.

CALENDARING AND BUILDING A WORK PLAN

Ever since I was a one woman shop at Rollins, I have used a task calendar that was divided monthly with a list of the major projects I was working on that month. It helped me stay focused, it helps communicate with others and it helps with my final point. It helps to stay at a high level for your projects; avoiding drilling down into the minutia of the tasks and becoming overwhelmed.

MAKE LISTS

I keep a weekly task list on my iPad that combines my work life, professional development life, and personal life into one. At work every Monday, I come into the office and make a task list of two sides, one of items that *need* to be completed this week and items that I *want* to have completed that week. I try to vary the list and, just like homework when I was in school, balance one thing I love doing with one thing I would rather not. Crossing things off the list helps keep me motivated and organized and works well when others want to place additional items on my plate.

HAVE A HEAT CHART

When I arrived at my one of my past positions, I was tasked with rebuilding a donor relations shop from the ground up, something I love doing and, now as a consultant, help others perform audits to find out where they are doing best and need improvement. I built a spreadsheet that listed the items that needed to be completed, then sat with my VP and had her place them in categories – low, medium, and high – and built a heat chart, color coding them by importance then shaded them green when complete. This tool helped me prioritize and has been very beneficial for me.

DO ONE THING REALLY WELL

Perfect something and move onto the next thing when you are in a small shop or shop of one, as life and work tasks can be so overwhelming. Now that I have a staff, I can still say the same except now add managing people to the list. My mantra when I work on my program is to take one thing each year, semester, quarter, and perfect it as much as possible, do it really well, be satisfied and move on to the next. You *cannot* do it all perfectly at once right away, but you *can* build incrementally, one bite at a time. I would rather be doing a few things really well than be a mess at it all because I can't task manage and/or I am overwhelmed.

MAKE BETTER USE OF YOUR TIME

This may be the tip you least want to hear, but it's true. My friend Pierre Khawand gives wonderful workshops, webinars, and has many resources (people-onthego.com) if you are using your time wisely and efficiently.

Because I am an extreme morning person, I head into the office early. The quiet of the office in the morning helps me obtain focus and, some days, I get more done before others get there than I do with my daily distractions once everyone arrives and my extroverted need to interact takes over. Hate mornings? Stay late for some quiet time in the office, too. It helps a great deal. Pierre also says that focused bursts of highly efficient work is another way to manage, and I agree. Put on some headphones and block off time on your calendar, interruption free.

ASK FOR HELP

This seems basic but often times is overlooked. There is no loss of pride from admitting that you we help. And it builds camaraderie. People will respect you, you won't waste your time struggling with a spreadsheet or task that would take you double the time of someone else, and you will find that others will ask you for help with areas you are the expert in. A win-win all around.

GET ORGANIZED

If you are like me, order some colored file folders and a label maker, index your shared drive, and get to work. Organizing your space one good time will help you work in the future and will save you time digging through files when someone needs something urgently.

I would also urge you to move paperless; our shared drive is organized and comprehensive. Everything I have in print is necessary; I never print emails. On average, I have 5-8 emails in my inbox. If there is no reason for you to have it in paper and it will cause clutter, don't keep it. Google docs and Dropbox are life saving apps. I have been able to save the day many times because I have things on hand digitally, in restaurants, airports, offices, everywhere, stored in the cloud, where they are secure, easily accessible, and portable.

SUPER SECRET AND FINAL TIP: SAY "NO"

So here will be the revelation for some of you. It is okay, good, in fact, to sometimes say "no." I know it seems contrary to everything we are and do, but it is necessary, not only for your sanity, but also for your success. You can't say "no" without purpose and strategy though, and sometimes no matter how hard you try to refuse, "yes" is the only answer.

However, I find that many professionals are overburdened and unable to prioritize because they are not strategic planners, have people pleasing disease (an essential component for donor relations), and at times have martyr complexes. Since I'm not a therapist and keep a couple psychologists in their nice offices and summer homes myself, I won't begin to analyze that part of the issue. What I will say is that if you have a plan, a calendar, a heat list, are purposeful in your work and actions, explaining the no and declaring it to be true is much easier and is often respected by your leadership. It is easy to tell someone, "Not now" or "Here is what I am working on right now, how would you like me to shift my plans?" They will respect your strategic thinking and help you prioritize or shift your planning. If you fear you will be fired, thought less of, or otherwise negatively affected by taking the time to say "no," I urge you to analyze your situation and yourself. Tough love time.

I hope these tips have opened your eyes, helped start you on a changed path or just reassured you that indeed, you are on the right track.

MISSION IMPOSSIBLE

LESSONS IN CRISIS PROJECT MANAGEMENT

I was once given the largest and most pressure-packed project I've had to manage.

How can I describe the particular hell I have been working on? Combined, my team and I, a core group of four, put in a solid 14+ hour workdays and countless hours on the train and at home reviewing the documents. There are a few key lessons that I learned during this crisis project management and I want to share them with you.

HAVE A PLAN

My plan started in the shower at 5:00 AM, trying to come up with a list of resources we would need and what it would take to get the job done. Then I broke that out and began to assign those parts to the staff I had that were best suited for that role. My task was primary project management and quality control, I had someone in charge of spreadsheets and data, someone in charge of logistics, and another in charge of obtaining supplies and general needs.

Dividing the work played to my staff's strengths and helped us have clear roles and responsibilities. My admins also enjoyed watching me take lunch orders and running to get coffee and soda when the caffeine and sugar had run out; no job was too big or too small for any of us, including me.

COMMUNICATION IS KEY

Every day twice a day, the leadership wanted written updates, so before these happened, we met as a team to ensure that we could give them sound updates of our progress. I was constantly on the phone or emailing those in charge ensuring they knew of our status, sanity, and progress.

BUILD RELATIONSHIPS

You need to have built relationships *before* the crisis or project hits your plate. My team worked tirelessly side by side, with the mantra of "We can do this." We reached out to our key contacts and pulled in every favor in the book to accomplish what my VP called "mission impossible."

BE CLEAR ABOUT YOUR OBSTACLES AND WHERE YOU NEED HELP

There were many obstacles to our success in this project (most of them were people). Every time I faced one, I went to the leaders, the ones who handed down the edict to "Git r done" and told them of my obstacle. Phone calls from "on high" were made and the obstacle disappeared. You must be truthful and non-dramatic and don't make this about you or the person; keep it project-focused.

BE PREPARED FOR THE UNEXPECTED

Mid-way through the project, another division decided that the project was "too much to handle" and dropped their portion back on my office. My staff was agile and focused, we already had a plan of attack for our work and enacted our plan for their division's portion seamlessly.

DON'T JUST VENT

One of the largest lessons came from someone in charge of our operations who I really look up to. I was at a breaking point due to a staff member in another division being uncooperative, so I thought I would go to her to vent. Instead,

I learned a valuable lesson: there is no point in venting if you don't want something done about it. 30 seconds later the uncooperative party was told in no uncertain terms to "get with the program." I didn't need to vent, I needed action, and this leader made me see and realize that my venting was unproductive whining.

HAVE QUALITY CONTROL STANDARDS

At the beginning of the project, we all sat down and addressed our biggest potential pitfall, a simple mistake made due to time and pressure constraints. We are all human, but there was no room for error. Everything was reviewed three times, with the final review being mine so I would own any errors. We found mistakes, corrected them, and moved forward.

MAKE YOUR EXPECTATIONS UP FRONT

I communicated to my team that everything else in our lives and work was no longer a priority. Lunches and breaks disappeared, chit-chat and socializing with others became mute, and we all just buckled down. To ease the tension, there was plenty of bad greasy food, loud 80s music, and horrible jokes at our own mistakes, but everyone in our unit and elsewhere knew this was our sole focus.

TENSIONS CAN AND WILL ERUPT

My associate director and I got into a spat. At the time, we were both overworked, frustrated, and on edge. Apologies were said, we cooled down, and the work continued. *It wasn't personal*; it was the geyser erupting, the pressure being released. But it actually helped push us forward. Crap happens; it is how you deal with it and where you go from there that is important. PS- she won the fight.

CELEBRATE!

We bought celebration candy and kept it in the fridge waiting for the moment that I had been waiting 7 days for, sending the email to the big bosses that we had accomplished the impossible. We danced, we sang, we hugged and high-fived, the sense of relief was palpable.

DEBRIEF

And later, we will did a post mortem to learn what we could have done better, how I could have been a better leader, and to review our accomplishment.

I hope this helps those of you when you are assigned those impossible projects in the future and reminds you of those times when you just weren't going to make it!

NEW YEAR, NEW IDEAS

MAKING A CONCIOUS EFFORT TO INNOVATE

As the end of the fiscal year quickly approached, I was thinking about what it meant to have a new year. At Yeshiva, I got to celebrate three each year: the Jewish new year, the calendar new year, and the fiscal new year. Try to keep that straight in your head.

The nice thing about the new fiscal year is that it often allows us to begin to think about or implement new ideas. The trouble with that is that, for many of us, innovation in our bureaucratic organizations can be very challenging and sometimes impossible.

If you are the kind of professional that is happy with the status quo, warning, this post isn't for you. This post is about how to become an advocate of innovation, someone who can then deliver that message to leadership with a vested interest.

For many years now I have been seen as a leading innovator in the field of development and donor relations. This didn't happen by accident, as I make a conscious effort to have innovation at the forefront of everything I am and everything I do. So below I will expound on a few key steps to success.

YOU MUST OWN BEING INNOVATIVE AND PLAN FOR TIME TO DO SO.

If you don't, no one else will. It is your job to look at a process and be able to ask the question: "How can I make this better?" That is the core of the innovative spirit. Set aside time in your busy schedules for innovation. If you don't, you will continue doing the same old things over and over.

UNDERSTAND INNOVATION

Innovation is when a good idea meets implementation. You must define what "better" looks like and how you will strive to achieve it. It is wonderful to have a visionary idea, but if it is not able to be implemented, what is the point?

DO A RISK VS. BENEFIT ANALYSIS

What is this? As my father would put it, "It's a pro/cons list, silly." You need to balance the equation and make sure that the new innovation is worth any risks involved. There is *nothing* wrong with calculated risks.

EMBRACE FAILURE

In fact, give it a big hug and a smooch! I learn more from my failures than I *ever* have from a success! We have to stop being afraid to fail, and I will put this in its simplest terms: if you fail, no one will die. Thankfully what we do is powerful and meaningful and does a great deal of good in the world. However, thankfully, we don't hold anyone's lives in our hands like say, uhm, a brain surgeon or rocket scientist.

INNOVATION IS POSSIBLE AT EVERY ORGANIZATION

I have yet to find a leader, both in my daily work and on my consulting trips, who, if you present them with solid ideas and a plan for implementation, does not want things to be better. If you are reading this and shaking your head saying, "You don't know my VP/boss," this thought is for you: maybe it is not your message, but it is the messenger.

Tough love, yes.

But it applies to everyone, even me. I talk candidly that I am not everyone's cup of tea. However I know my strengths and weaknesses and often have other people present my ideas to leadership because I know that they are the right person to perform the approach. In football, it's called an end-around; in the military, it's called flanking. Take your pick!

CHECK YOUR EGO AT THE DOOR

Finally, and most importantly, innovation is not about you. If the idea gets credited to a lunar eclipse or to another team member, who cares!? It makes the organization better. If you are working in non-profit and don't understand that by now, get a job in the for-profit sector. I will happily let anyone take credit for any idea I come up with if it benefits us all in the end. Then, I quietly go back to my office and give myself a high five, add the innovation to my resume, and move on to the next!

BARS AND WEBINARS

IDEAS FOR PROFESSIONAL DEVELOPMENT

I believe that for your professional development dollars, there is no better investment than a conference. One might ask two questions though:

1. What is so great about a conference other than the sessions; and,

2. If I don't have conference budget money, what can I do?

So here we go- tips and tricks from your guru friend.

CONFERENCES ARE NOT ALL ABOUT THE SESSIONS

True, those of us that speak would like you to believe that our educational offerings are the end-all, be-all, but in reality, it just isn't true. I often learn more outside of the sessions than I do in them. Here's how: I am constantly networking. There is no better teacher than hundreds or even thousands of people who do the same thing you do for a living. The shared bonds there are priceless and when you need a second or third opinion, what a great resource!

TALK TO THE VENDORS

Most of the conference vendors are great industry resources and have been around a while. They have a perspective that some of us cannot grasp, as we are so deeply entrenched in the day-to-day.

SPEND TIME AT THE BAR OR PLAN AN OUTING

I'm not encouraging you to drink – well, maybe – but ginger ale is perfectly acceptable here. Most of the leaders like to unwind at the end – or sometimes even in the middle – of the day with a good glass of wine or single malt scotch! If you catch someone there, the conversations can be very beneficial to your educational path and your career trajectory. Some of the best hiring deals are done at the bar!

Not a drinker? Sign up for a dinner group or make one of your own! It doesn't take much effort to have a great time with colleagues and learn more about them. Staying in your conference hotel room will do you no good! You might say, "Well I want to see X city." Great! Add a day for that. You are there to get development, and the best way is from your peers and industry leaders.

SET UP VISITS

If you have extra time and are in an area with lots of non-profits, set up lunches or visits to places and people you would like to visit, both formally or informally. Use every minute of your time away from the office to develop your skills and learn from others. Be thrilled with the fact that your organization is providing you with a wonderful opportunity to be present and engaged in a conference! Don't forget to write follow up emails and thank you notes to those you met and spent time with, it will leave a lasting impression!

Do you have no budget money to travel to a conference? Here are some great ideas for those of you that are landlocked for the time being.

APPLY FOR A SCHOLARSHIP

Most conferences I attend have scholarship programs and are always looking for wonderful applicants. Go for it!

FOLLOW THE CONFERENCE YOU WANT TO ATTEND ON SOCIAL MEDIA

Particularly Twitter. It is amazing how much you can learn from us tweeps as we live tweet or blog sessions. It is like you are there...almost! You can ask questions, follow along, and even reach out to speakers live!

REACH OUT TO SPEAKERS

When you find a speaker you like and see slides that interest you from one of their speeches – most can be found on slideshare.net or their websites – reach out to them, explaining you weren't able to be there in person, but you wanted to see if they could talk you through it. I've never said "no" to anyone and have learned a great deal from these one-on-one sessions. Don't forget to send them a thank you note afterward!

SIGN UP FOR A WEBINAR

Webinars are a cost-effective solution to your inability to travel. They are often hosted by the same speakers and have wonderful content. Some organizations even include them in their annual membership fee.

HELP ORGANIZE A REGIONAL WORKSHOP

Volunteer locally! It doesn't cost you anything but time and you usually can attract top speakers to your location. It is a great selling point to your leadership that they might want to let you attend the national version of that conference once they see the value of the sessions and networking that day!

READ!

There are some great blogs out there...*ahem*...

Newspapers such as the *Chronicle of Philanthropy*, websites and other sources for you to feel engaged in the larger community while still at your desk!

PARTICIPATE

Use social media and other forms of sharing like listservs to have your burning questions answered. Every major group has a LinkedIn and/or Facebook page, and most have Twitter feeds. There is a lot to be discussed and learned out there and each of these are FREE.

AND IF JIMMY JUMPS OFF A CLIFF?

ARE YOU CHALLENGING ASSUMPTIONS?

I enjoy receiving emails from folks all over the world asking for advice. I do my best to answer them within 24 hours and ensure I give real life advice from my experiences and based on best and next practices.

Here is an example of an email that suggests to me that sometimes we have a larger problem facing us.

> *My supervisor said that Non-profit X is doing (insert horrible practice here) and that we should do it, too.*

Le Sigh. Just because another organization does it or that it worked in one instance doesn't mean it's best practice or even a legal practice.

Here are some of the examples I've read lately that make my stomach flip:

- Putting a business reply envelope in with the receipt

- Withholding scholarship money from a student because they didn't write a note to a donor

- Giving an acrylic tchotcke/paperweight to a donor with their name inscribed on it for their deferred gift

- Putting the link to the giving website on every single communication

- Ignoring donor retention numbers and instead only focusing on alumni participation

Like your mother said growing up, "Just because Jimmy jumps off a cliff, are you going to do it, too?" I think that there are a few horrible reasons to do something in the non-profit sector and here is my "hit list":

- We've always done it that way

- "So and So" does this

- One of our donors says they like it

- XX Vendor says it works for them at XX organization

How are you challenging assumptions? Are you using guiding principals to help you make decisions? When something doesn't feel right, are you questioning it? I have to tell you that if you let data drive your efforts, some of these pitfalls are easy to avoid. Also, your general counsel and others can help you stay out of a danger zone as well. We all want to do better for our organizations. If we didn't we wouldn't be in this industry. We care about our mission, about our supporters, about our work.

So why do we succumb to these pressures? Because we aren't always provided with wonderful alternatives. We have to be advocates for our donors and supporters. Remember, if it doesn't benefit the donor, we shouldn't be doing it.

Help me help you fight the good fight and question authority. It's perfectly acceptable to reason something out and use empirical evidence rather than anecdotal evidence.

THE HARDEST PART OF THE JOB

TIPS FOR MANAGING PEOPLE

People often ask me what the most difficult thing I do is, and for me, and for many of you, it's always the same answer:

It's the people.

I can juggle many complex tasks, organize an event for tomorrow, listen to an irate donor until I've lulled them to happiness, and crank out work like you wouldn't believe. But the thing that keeps me up at night, other than my nightmares of angry talking tchotchkes, is managing people.

I'm not just speaking of direct reports or a specific department, but managing people in all directions is not only difficult, but at times draining. For those of you that have the whole people thing down pat, congratulations, but I've never met you. For the rest of us, some things I have learned.

HIRE WELL

If you have the chance, hire well, hire to your weaknesses, and then get out of the way. The pool of development talent can sometimes seem shallow and murky. Two written-in-stone rules for me:

1. Don't hire anyone in development with a mistake on their résumé, no matter how small, and

2. Don't hire anyone who doesn't write you a hand-written note after you interview them. Nope, email isn't good enough; they need to understand the power of a note.

TRY TO MANAGE EXPECTATIONS, NOT JUST PEOPLE

This one works well for me, as I am a very direct personality. This works especially well when managing up or someone who may not understand exactly what it is you do. Set a clear understanding of the outcomes, deadlines, action items, what you need, and if you're not in charge, you can always clarify in a follow up communication, enhancing your listening skills and their consciousness of your presence in the process. Don't be a martyr. Be a powerful professional instead.

UNDERSTAND THAT NOT EVERYONE LEARNS OR COMMUNICATES IN THE SAME WAY YOU DO.

I am an email first person, it is my safety zone for communication and I love data, spreadsheets, and crunching numbers. Some people prefer face-to-face communication and charts (those two seem to go together for some reason) or phone calls and anecdotes. Learn about your audience and help adapt your style to them. Want it in writing? Good, you can always send a follow up email.

In the same hand, hard to believe, but when someone shows you who they are, believe them. Most people are incapable of large sweeping change – hence the reason most New Years resolutions fail miserably – but people can adapt. I can never change who I am at the core of my existence, and I'm okay with that, but I have learned to adapt or not, depending on the circumstance and consequence.

How can you help someone adapt to you? For me, I try to disarm people with humor because I know I'm a big personality, and I also explain that I enjoy direct feedback.

BE THE KIND OF BOSS AND COWORKER YOU WANT

I have learned great lessons from my many leaders. But my first leadership and management lesson was taught to me by my Dad.

We were walking through one of the massive factories he ran when I was little and he greeted everyone by name, but stopped to chat with the janitor (now called a sanitation engineer). I asked him why he took special time for that man and he said to me, "Because I used to be a janitor. They know everything and are the heart of the operation. Treat them well and you can't fail." No truer words were ever spoken.

We tend to get caught up in titles and hierarchy, especially in Higher Ed. The titles I choose to focus on are names, regardless of what they do.

HIRE WELL

Sounds like a repeat, huh? Nope. Ask good questions during the interview process and observe behaviors that aren't direct, like how people treat support staff, servers in restaurants, etc. Also note how difficult they make it to schedule time with them. Some of my favorite interview questions that I've asked or have been asked of me:

- What does philanthropy mean to you?

- What kind of work fulfills you?

- Tell me the last book you read.

- When was the last time you made a mistake?

- Tell me about a time when you were a doer and a time when you were a thinker or observer.

- What has been your greatest learning experience on the job?

BE MORE STOIC

If you don't have anything nice to say, come sit next to me. Just kidding; this is a quote from *Steel Magnolias*. But the thing I struggle with daily is learning to be more stoic (otherwise known as a poker face) and more quiet in meetings. This will be a lifelong struggle for me, but I am getting much better. Doodling helps...seriously. But sometimes you can't help but be quiet because its best to not open your mouth. For those of you that have mastered this, let's hang out in silence together.

UNDERSTAND HUMANNESS

We're not perfect, but we sure are interesting. Not everyone was made to be friends, but we can all try to work together in harmony. If you can't seem to make it work, look at yourself first and then ask someone you respect to help you. Some personalities are just not a good mix, no matter how hard you try. So you may have to bless and release some things.

BENCH MARKING FORM AND ETIQUETTE

HELP INCREASE YOUR RESPONSE RATE

BY DEBBIE MEYERS

Like many things in life, bench marking has its good points and bad points. On the one hand, after hours of research and analysis, it may end up telling you what you already know or nothing you need to know. But it can also provide you with an idea or two about how to proceed with your project, or validation that you are indeed doing the right things the right way.

And let's face it: sometimes we don't have a choice. The boss says bench mark, so we bench mark. End of story.

Regardless of your situation, here are some questions you should consider asking yourself before you start your bench marking journey.

WHAT AM I TRYING TO FIND OUT, EXACTLY?

Sound like a big "duh"? Not really. A common request for information involves giving societies, where we are asked to help the bench marker "understand how peer institutions establish various levels of giving and the respective benefits for each level." It may be semantics, but I don't think that's what you want to understand.

To find out what you're trying to find out, ask yourself that question, several times, until you are crystal clear on your task. Your conversation with yourself may go something like this:

Q: Why am I asking other organizations about levels and benefits?

A: To see how they do it.

Q: Why?

A: Because I want to make sure I'm following Best Practices. (In capitals, because it is now the holy shrine at which everyone in our profession now worships as we strive to take our programs to the Next Level – but that's a topic for another day.)

Q: Why?

A: So I can ultimately figure out how make my donors feel recognized and appreciated.

AHA! Now you've got the right answer. If that's the true reason, then why not ask your donors what would make them feel recognized and appreciated? But let's say you need some validation that you're on the right track in your levels and benefits. Remember that your focus should be on your donors, not the inner workings of the institutions you're querying.

DO I HAVE THE RIGHT POOL TO BENCH MARK AGAINST?

So your boss says, "Call XYZ University – everyone says they have an awesome donor relations program."

But is XYZ the right fit? If I'm a small private institution, will I care about or benefit from how a large public institution does things, regardless of how awesome their program is or how many stewardship rock stars run their show? My levels are based on MY donors; your levels should be based on YOUR donors. Run the numbers and see where the logical groupings are.

Benefits don't benefit anyone unless they are meaningful. Some donors want parking. Others want preferred seating at events. We are apples and oranges. So what kind of oranges would your donors like?

Identify institutions whose mission, size, staffing and donor base are as close to yours as possible. It never hurts to throw in some others, for they may provide you with some good ideas or aspirations. But your most meaningful data will be from your peer group.

AM I ASKING THE RIGHT QUESTIONS IN A USER-FRIENDLY FORMAT?

The best way to get an answer is to keep your questions simple and clear. That may sound obvious, but you'd be surprised how many questions I get that require me to pull data or analyze a report. If you want a timely and accurate response, keep it simple.

You may want to include an example, for clarity and consistency: something like, "We do it this way. How do you do it?" Having a mix of open-ended and closed-ended questions will most likely give you more information, and certainly more context.

Also, have someone outside your department read the questions to make sure you haven't been in your own little world too long with this project.

WOULD MISS MANNERS APPROVE?

Remember who's doing who the favor. Professional courtesy is a wonderful thing, and many will respond to your survey just because they are professionally courteous, but it has to go both ways to work.

Take a few minutes to make your introduction warm, friendly and informational: here's who I am, here's what I'm trying to do, why and here's why I chose you. (Great opportunity to flatter the responder!) Sometimes including one survey to a group, and letting everyone in the group see who else is in the group, greases the skids in a way that one-on-one doesn't.

Make it easy for your responders to reply. Ask their preference in answering by phone or email. If your questions lend themselves to a Survey Monkey format, all the better. If by phone, let them know how long it will take. Offer to share results once the survey is completed. That gives them an incentive to participate and shows that you are invested in the project's success. Include a response deadline, and offer to be available if they have questions.

MOST IMPORTANTLY, DO YOUR HOMEWORK.

If one of your questions is something common like endowment minimums or naming opportunities, check the institution's website and see if that information is already available. And do let the person know in the intro that you have already done that. You will earn huge brownie points.

After you finish and send the survey results back, it's a nice touch to add a short summary of what you learned, ending the process on a positive note.

MA'AM, THE POTPOURRI IS NOT EDIBLE

WHAT TO DO WHEN YOU MAKE A MISTEAK...ER...MISTAKE

Yesterday, I had an F+ kind of day. We all have them, and because we're human, we're not perfect, gasp! So I thought I would write about what to do when the good goes bad (much cheaper than seeing my therapist).

Most of what I learned about how to deal with failure, I learned from others, both what to do and what not to do. When you embrace risk, you must also learn to embrace failure. Part of the reason why so few things change is the fear of failure. So here are my tips on how to fail upward.

NO MATTER WHAT, STAY CALM

We can learn this lesson from many people who have nerves of steel in the worst situations. We can also learn this from watching someone panic aimlessly. When a donor slides most ungracefully down a set of concrete stairs in the pouring rain (it always happens in the *worst* weather) and begins to bleed, calmly call 911, and then go sit next to the person and calmly talk to them in the rain, dress, heels, makeup, and all until help arrives. Panicking doesn't help anyone, and believe me, you can't make it look good, so don't try.

MAKE LEMONADE

The next lesson came to me from my first Vice President and mentor, Cynthia Wood. I was called to fill in unexpectedly for her Executive Assistant and the first morning within my first hour I took a call for her from the Chairman of the Board's wife. When I went to transfer it to Cynthia, yup, I hit the wrong button...

Poof! Call gone!

Cynthia didn't hesitate or take the time to berate me, she picked up the phone, dialed Mrs. Board Chairman's wife and quickly said in jest, "You hung up on me!" She saved me, and made lemonade out of lemons. We never spoke of it, but I'll never forget it.

It taught me a great lesson about leadership and about making a mistake. Instead of wasting her time yelling at me, she just fixed the problem. When you've done something wrong, or when failure happens, work like hell to make it right or to compensate in a meaningful manner. It's not just good donor relations, but it's the right thing to do.

FALL ON YOUR SWORD

My friend Debbie taught me a great lesson about falling on my sword and personal accountability. When you mess up, take the blame by putting on some of those big 80s shoulder pads and fall on your sword. Admit it, apologize, and move on. In that order. The order there is important. A little humility goes a long way. I like to insert a step in there about venting. After this episode of venting, I'll be moving on.

PARK THE BUS

My friend and mentor Dawn also taught me a good one: being a Martyr is unflattering, but throwing someone else under the bus leaves tire tracks on you, too. It's okay not to blame everyone in the universe when something goes wrong. It's completely acceptable to figure out what went wrong as a process, but not as a means to place blame. When the crucial conversation needs to happen, make sure it's in private and not public. Dawn always wore a bullet proof vest in public for her team, and never yelled or criticized in public to embarrass or demean. I can't tell you how invaluable that is, especially when you've experienced the opposite. Being humiliated or chastised in "mixed company" – as my Southern friends call it – is unforgettable and something you will remember not to do given the chance.

DON'T REPEAT YOUR MISTAKES

My parents get credit for the next one: don't repeat your mistake. Doing the same thing again and again and expecting a different result just doesn't work. I think Einstein called it the definition of instanity. You'll never see me giving away or having potpourri at an event after watching a tipsy older donor eat it in front of my eyes because she thought it was snack mix; bark, orange rinds, and all. No Sir. I won't be repeating that mistake again. You think I'm kidding, but I'm not. Really, we all have one of those stories, don't we?

EMBRACE FAILURE, CELEBRATE IT EVEN

When I worked at Disney World – yup, pixie dust and all – we had a "Jean-ius" trophy we would pass back and forth amongst the kitchen staff for the person who was the "smartest" that week. Basically it was an award for having the worst week. It was an ugly trophy, but vastly meaningful. Because if you can't laugh about forgetting to add the sugar to an entire batch of 1,000 sugar cookies, who can?

REALIZE IT'S NOT LIFE AND DEATH

Fortunately for the vast majority of us in the fundraising world, if we make a mistake, no one dies. Usually, that is. I am appreciative for a job in which no one's life is in my hands on a daily basis. Because it's not life and death, we should have the ability to make mistakes, fail upward and land okay, bruises and all. As a manager, you have to let that happen, too, sometimes, even when you can see it ahead. In my entire life, I have learned more from my mistakes than the rest of my experiences combined.

SHAKE IT OFF

Thank you, Taylor Swift! Shake it off and land on your feet like a cat. Resiliency is a great human trait, just like imperfection... Most of us don't know just how resilient we are until truly knocked askew. Be like Gumby and bounce back even better!

SHAKING THE SNOW GLOBE

AND OTHER CHANGE MANAGEMENT TECHNIQUES FOR SUCCESS

Change is the only constant.

The non-profit world seems to be in a hesitant state of maintenance, a vast veil of denial that holds it back from true progress. We seem to be an industry steeped and mired in tradition, often for no other reason than "we've always done it that way". As a change agent in my chosen career it can often be maddening to explain to people the obvious, that not only are we behind, but we avoid change at a clear and obvious detriment to ourselves and the causes we serve.

When I first started my career I was a big proponent of rocking the boat and ripping-the-bandaid-off type of change management. They work, they really do...they will just get you more comfortable with the guest chairs in HR and senior leadership offices than anyone really needs. HR always goes for the soothing fabric, by the way.

So over the past few years I have replaced the shock-and-awe technique with one I call "Shaking the Snow Globe." What that means is that, much like a snow globe, all of the buildings stay the same, but the environment around it changes. This theory of change management is much less scary to those who abhor change the way many non-profits do. Here are some of my guidelines for how to effect change in a daily, sustainable way that provides a much more successful result.

FIND YOUR CHEERLEADERS

No, not the ones in short skirts waving pom-poms. This is important when your idea is new to an organization, buy in is crucial, fortunately you don't need it from everyone. Find some key influencers, find those who are of a similar mindset and have them help you do the tricky work of presenting an idea. With a chorus of well placed yeses, it goes over much more smoothly.

THE TRUTH HURTS

This one is true more often than not. When you point out the obvious, there are several reactions, defensiveness, stupor, hurt feelings, and rage. You have to be prepared for all of these, and prepared to let the dust settle before moving forward. It's perfectly acceptable to tell the truth all of the time, I've learned it's in the art of the delivery. Some people need a wake up via cold water on the face, others need to hit the snooze button a few times before they're vertical. Either way, the truth will come, can you be patient enough for the epiphanies?

FEEDBACK AND EVIDENCE IS VITAL TO SUCCESS

Especially if the feedback comes from donors: get your rubber ducks in a row before you present upward. Remember evidence and bench marking is vital to success. Also, empirical evidence doesn't hurt. Remember this the next time someone asks you for the latest in paperweights or ugly neck ties! Do your homework and have the facts easily at hand. For senior leadership, make some pretty charts and graphs.

DON'T ARGUE WITH CRAZY

Seriously. Understand that with some folks you have to bless and release, or as they say in the South, "Bless your heart." Some people will never be on board with a new idea, even if it helps them, and that's okay; we're gonna have to let that go. Arguing with crazy makes you look bad, and no one wants to pick on the kid that just can't help it. Now if the crazy is at the top of the food chain, that's a bit tougher.

DON'T ACCEPT NO FROM A PERSON WHO COULD NEVER HAVE GIVEN YOU A YES ANYWAY

This is a great tip for those of you who call customer service. When the only answer is "no," try to find someone who *can* give you a "yes." Is IT telling you that automating something is impossible? Have you asked your peer institutions? Have you asked the software company? Sometimes a no comes from ignorance of the possibilities and sometimes it comes from a "That's above my pay grade" mentality, and sometimes it comes from folks who just don't know what's possible or probable. That's when I kindly say, "Supervisor" into the phone.

IF YOU TRY AND FAIL, THAT'S BETTER THAN SETTLING FOR "WE'VE ALWAYS DONE IT THAT WAY"

Failing upward is an art form. How can you practice the art if you don't try? After banging your head against the desk for a while, you'll realize that it hurts. So, other than a concussion, what hopefully occurs is the realization that you own the responsibility to make it better, to effect change, to help others see the way.

As a culture, non-profit is behind and always playing catch up, how do we rectify this without change? We can't. Calculated risk taking should be more encouraged and appreciated, but it starts with every one of us.

What will you do today to help embrace change?

DUCT TAPE ON A BUMPER, BAND-AID ON AN AMPUTATION

COSTLY SHORT-SIGHTED THINKING

Growing up, my Dad always taught me that once a car had been in an accident, no matter how good the repair, you don't want to drive it again. Instead, spend the money and get a new car that hasn't been in an accident. His reasoning became so clear one night around 11:00 PM at the top of a hill when my newly repaired car died because of a wiring problem that was overlooked during the body repairs to it. I appreciated his advice as the city bus bore down on me in my stalled car even more and I ran for the hills. It's like that in our industry, too, with short-sided thinking costing us more in the end than the initial expense that no one wants to swallow.

So here's the thing I've noticed a great deal about non-profits: we tend to plan and run at the same time, often with damaging results. Think about it in terms of growing up; you were always told not to run with scissors and pencils, it can get pointy. It's just a short-term model of thinking that has a few drawbacks, among them: it can be costly both financially and in human resources, its short-sided and doesn't allow for long term strategy, and it does not benefit the organization in a directed strategic manner.

We see this far too often in donor relations and particularly events. Lack of prior planning turns into emergencies and hastily done projects at the expense of the greater good. People are newly hired (sometimes without the proper training or background of skills) and upon their laps is laid all of the responsibilities of building a program, all at once. Oh, and by the way, with limited or no resources.

Instead, I always advise folks to take one project, plan and do it really well, hone and refine it, and then move on to the next task. It isn't just frustrating; it's dangerous. In the rush, large and small details can be overlooked that can truly be costly. It is much better to spend a little time and money up front than try to fix the problem later. You end up spending more time and money in the end, and in the meantime, there can be large amounts of frustration and waste.

So how do we solve this problem?

We can be a force of change, a voice of reason and a resource for those who need true problem solving. I have my reputation in the industry as a fixer for a reason (think Olivia Pope for you *Scandal* fans). It's called the STAR approach:

- I can come in, assess the **SITUATION** when I arrive...

- ...build **TASKS** to help solve the problem...

- ...define the **ACTIONS** taken...

- ...and express the **RESULTS**.

But I go a step further and have people understand what could have prevented this in the first place. We learn how to avoid these emergencies that need fixing and build enhanced thought processes for the future. It's a valuable and important skill.

The other half of that fixing is the willingness to be able to be a vocal advocate before the train wreck happens. I'm okay with being the one to speak up and voice concerns. You can't be afraid. You have to take a risk by opening your mouth and not letting mediocrity happen. But when you do, make sure you have the data to back it up. Make sure you don't just voice a problem; you also bring three solutions with you as well. The more you do this, the more valuable you will become in the process and the organization.

Help people set boundaries and proper strategic planning. You can be very effective by helping folks invest in infrastructure, plan using cost analysis, and be strategic in their decision making. And when you plan for costs, by all means, demonstrate that spending $4,000 up front is actually much cheaper than spending $8,000 in two years.

I'm happy to help people solve problems; I'm a fixer. But I'm also a strategic planner, and would rather avoid those pressure-packed situations where I'm scrambling for a solution and wiping sweat off of my brow, then exhaling when they work. Hyper-focused fixing is just planning in the short term, taking the whole strategic process, and condensing it.

ANECDOTAL vs EMPIRICAL DONOR EVIDENCE

WHICH ONE DRIVES YOUR STRATEGY?

Sitting at an airport gate is a lot like looking at a donor spreadsheet. You never know what you're going to see. I'm sitting at a gate waiting for a flight and it's the best people watching ever. But I can only tell you what I hear and observe. All of that is filtered through my cynical, I-travel-too-much, snarky lens.

It's the same way for you and your donors. I can't tell you how many times I sit down with clients and I ask them why they're doing something the way they are and often times I hear this:

> *One time a donor (insert name here) said that they either did or didn't like it and so because of that we do it this way,*

We spend a lot of time dispelling myths and debunking those one-off stories. We in the fundraising world tend to believe that as the gospel truth and then run with it. What many of us fail to realize is that those are the outliers, you know, like the lady who is sitting at the gate having a conversation with herself about how much she misses TWA.

Far too often we plan for the minority and the majority suffers. We take those stories at their face value and never doubt the source behind them. Instead, we can combat this with qualitative and empirical data. I go back to my point of comprehensive donor and alumni surveys and feedback mechanisms.

I once headed out to a client to present their survey data, and boy was it a gold mine! After pouring over more than 1,500 responses, I've found their medians, their donors desired and needs, and figured out what they were doing well and what needed to improve. And of course, there were the outliers, like the guy who hated the pickles in the cafeteria (I think he's TWA lady's future spouse). But we can now build an entire plan based on real data and analyze it for the deep truths buried within.

No longer will they have to rely on stories and one-offs to control their strategy. They have all the evidence they need. If you haven't done a comprehensive study recently, why not? How do you build your program without data? As you begin to fly the friendly (bumpy) skies of change, make sure you have real evidence to guide you as you make strategic decisions for the future.

READY, AIM, AIM, AIM

TIPS FOR MAKING DECISIONS

As donor relations and fundraising professionals, we are often faced with many decisions, some of them in rapid-fire succession. I love decision making, for the most part, and I find it is what defines me. I am able to quickly assess a situation and make a decision that can turn the tide and create change. One of my alumni board members enjoys the way I'm able to make "executive decisions" and quickly delineate the direction in which we should head. I consider all of the facts as they are presented to me and then forge a path ahead.

That said, it seems like decision making is really easy for me. It is far from easy, I've just honed my skills in this area so I can help my organization and many others move forward. Far too often non-profits are paralyzed by decision making. We find ourselves making the mistake of decision by committee, or we make no decision at all, sort of like ready, aim...

....aim...aim...aim...aim...

...and we never get to fire.

Decision making isn't easy by a long shot, we live in a world of grey areas and I am definitely a black-and-white girl. So here are some of the tools I use to help me make decisions and help others to do so as well.

- I always start with a simple foundation of ethics. Does this feel smarmy to me? Is there a gray area I'm not ethically comfy with? If so, decision is made, avoid it!

- I tend to try to take the emotion and the person out of the decision. Don't make decisions based on people or emotions. It will always cloud your judgment.

- My mantra remains: If it doesn't benefit the alumni or the donors, we don't do it. You'll never go wrong.

- Respect the hierarchy and rank of your organization. If the decision involves someone who is truly above your pay grade, your considerations are amplified.

- Make a pros and cons list. It's a simple yet effective way to determine the ROI and the impact of your decision. I have these everywhere. I've gotten so good at this I can do it in my head.

- Go to people you trust and ask them for their opinion, especially those who are your mentors or work in your industry, but not directly in your organization. That outside opinion is so valuable that I use it often. Even if sometimes you feel like you are venting, you're really seeking advice. Tap into that network!

- Ask someone who thinks completely differently from you how they would handle it. I'm not exactly known for my huge glug of empathy, so I tend to balance my opinion with that of others who know the softer side, those who think people and emotions first, not systems, strategy, and process first. I find they help me think about things I wouldn't have otherwise.

- Trust your gut. Think with your head, especially at work, but don't deny what your heart and gut tell you, especially in the case of human resources. You and only you know what the right decision is, and there's nothing wrong with trusting your gut, your first instinct is usually correct.

HERE'S A NEW IDEA

ADAPTING SOMEONE ELSE'S IDEA
TO MAKE IT YOURS

I'm often asked how to come up with the latest innovation or new concept in fundraising. Here's a secret: I haven't had a new idea in a decade! Just kidding. But in all reality I think that one of the most important things we can learn is how to take an existing idea from another organization and adapt it for use in our environment. There is no reason to reinvent the wheel, but you can always put new tires on that baby.

I think one of the best things about our industry is the open sharing and cross-pollination of strong networks. I have never picked up the phone or sent an email to someone asking for them to share their work or use their idea and adapt it and heard the word "no."

What does it take to adapt a new idea and make it yours? Here's the steps I usually follow to find the latest and greatest.

READ, PARTICIPATE, AND ATTEND!

Read blogs, websites, social media to see what others are doing and to find some great samples. CASE, Fundsvcs, SupportingAdvancement, and other sites have great samples! Twitter and SlideShare contain tons of examples as well. Participate in group sharing by adding your samples for others to see. Send out your items and when you do, you will receive more in return. And finally attend as many professional development opportunities as possible. Conferences have tables of swaps, AFP chapters have tons of sharing resources, as do others.

FIND SOMETHING YOU LIKE?

Email or call the office of the people who created it and talk to them about it. Most people will be so flattered and can help you with the strengths of their process and the pitfalls to avoid. Then send them a thank you note for their time and always credit them if the idea is originally theirs. Sometimes you'll find out they stole it from someone else, too!

HAVING TROUBLE WITH A CONCEPT?

Lean on the expert resources you have. Take the samples you acquire directly to your communications or marketing team of designers to show them exactly what you want. They can help you brainstorm how to apply that idea to your organization. I keep an entire folder in my Dropbox of screenshots of wonderful things I've seen and want to implement some day and I also have a binder of clear sleeves housing work I admire as well. Pinterest can be a great tool, as well. These inspiration collections help me greatly when the dreaded blank state happens.

LEADERSHIP vs MANAGEMENT

WHAT IS YOUR LEADERSHIP STYLE?

I've spent a great deal of time recently helping lead my new team. I've done this in a variety of ways, leading by example, setting high standards, and providing accountability. I've been thinking a great deal about my leadership style and how in the past, the team wasn't led, they were managed.

There exists a large chasm between management and leadership. If you've ever experienced them both, you know the difference is palpable. Management consists of controlling a group or a set of entities to accomplish a goal. Leadership refers to an individual's ability to influence, motivate, and enable others to contribute toward organizational success. Influence and inspiration separate leaders from managers, not power and control.

Management is a set of well-known processes, like planning, budgeting, structuring and staffing jobs, problem-solving, and measuring performance, which help an organization to predictably do what it knows how to do well. Management helps you to produce products and services as you have promised, of consistent quality, on budget, day after day, week after week. In organizations of any size and complexity, this is an enormously difficult task. We constantly underestimate how complex this task really is, especially if we are not in senior management jobs. You can't lead and micromanage at the same time. If you do, you must be exhausted.

So management is crucial — but it's not leadership.

Leadership is entirely different. It is associated with taking an organization into the future, finding opportunities that are coming at it faster and faster, and successfully exploiting those opportunities. Leadership is about vision, about people buying in, about empowerment and, most of all, about producing useful change. Leadership is not about attributes, but rather about behavior.

In an ever-faster-moving world, leadership is increasingly needed from more and more people, no matter where they are in a hierarchy. The notion that a few extraordinary people at the top can provide all the leadership needed today is ridiculous, and it's a recipe for failure.

Many people, by the way, are both. They have management jobs, but they realize that you cannot buy hearts, especially to follow them down a difficult path, and so act as leaders, too. I'm a great project manager, I do whatever it takes to get the job done, but I love to lead along the way. Managers are at times, leaders, so the paradox never ends. Your task is to adopt the correct style when either leading or managing.

WADITWA DISEASE

WE'VE ALWAYS DONE IT THAT WAY

Non-profit organizations seem to be diametrically opposed to change. My friend Mary always says that one of our greatest problems we face as a profession is overcoming the resistance of our organizations to change. Let's face it, many of us are solidly stuck in the 1980s when it comes to change management. We suffer from WADITWA disease: We've Always Done It That Way.

But how do we overcome the obstacle of tradition in our profession and allow for progress?

We ourselves must be fearless in the pursuit of evaluating what is currently working, pushing for best in class programs and making a future for ourselves and our donors. Let's face it, most of our donors work in industries that have fully embraced the new millennium and beyond. Yet when they interact with us, they are driven back into the stone age by being respectful to our "traditions." To this, I say that there has to be a better way.

One challenge is that being a risk taker in a traditional environment isn't always rewarded or applauded. When it happens and when we embrace calculated risk and change, the results can be remarkable. Charity:Water is a great example of a non-profit that embraces the new different and challenges the status quo and they've been very successful doing it.

I find it ironic that non-profit organizations' missions are tied directly to changing the world they're in, yet they resist change at every turn (cue Alanis Morrisette here). Is it because we lack the resources to affect change? Nope, not a good excuse. Is it because our leadership is risk adverse? Not necessarily, when I come in as a consultant I find leadership most welcoming to new ideas have sound reasoning behind them.

So what is it that gives us the WADITWA disease?

Is a cultural shift in non-profits that difficult? I don't think so. Is now not the right time? Nope, carpe diem! Let's together stop making, accepting and allowing excuses to get in the way of fantastic progress. I'm here to help, provide resources, and challenge your status quo. Join me as we venture forth bravely to banish WADITWA and all that comes with it. We must be the torchbearers for change from within our organizations.

STUCK ON THE TARMAC

IDEAS WITHOUT IMPLEMENTATION

As many of you know, my formula for innovation is:

A great idea + Implementation = Innovation

So what happens when you've been presented with many new ideas – let's say at a conference or webinar – but with no way to implement? You end up in a holding pattern or stuck on the tarmac unable to take off. As many of us who travel know, that's no fun! After lots of frustration, you reach your final destination, but wonder about all of the time you lost along the way, and how close your were to running out of fuel.

So how do you arrive at implementation from an idea?

The first part is about not only receiving the idea, but what that would look like in the reality of your organization. Do I have the resources, time, budget, and buy in? Is this something my audience would appreciate or am I doing this because I can (bad idea)? Who am I aiming to please? Because if the answer there is just leadership or yourself, stop now!

I say all of this not from my usual subway car, but a comfy bed in a conference hotel where ideas fly throughout (most) sessions and the bright shiny things amaze us. What good is it to have – or steal – a bright shiny one if it doesn't work?

Nail the idea folks down. Not literally of course, that would hurt. But ask, the HOW. How is very important in implementation, even more so than the why. We know why, because we thought it was a good idea and would benefit our audience, right? But how did you implement it? What did your planning process look like (sometimes what just sneaks right in there)? How did you fight for the resources? How did you get buy in across the organization?

Everyone needs a flight plan, where the rubber meets the road – or should I say wings meet the air? That plan begins with the idea and ends with an evaluation of whether or not the end result was worth it. Don't forget that step! It's not good enough to declare it a success because it's new, you have to assess the worth. This may take time; we don't want to throw away something until we've given it enough time for the journey. But at all costs, as mentioned in the previous chapter, we want to avoid our new idea WADITWA disease.

APPENDIX

MY FAVORITE GRATITUDE QUOTES

I can no other answer make but thanks, and thanks, and ever thanks...

– William Shakespeare
Twelfth Night, Act III, scene III

"It takes a noble man to plant a seed for a tree that will someday give shade to people he may never meet."

– D.E. Trueblood

Silent gratitude isn't much use to anyone.

– G.B. Stern

I would maintain that thanks are the highest form of thought, and that gratitude is happiness doubled by wonder.

– G.K. Chesterton

I feel a very unusual sensation - if it is not indigestion, I think it must be gratitude.

– Benjamin Disraeli

Hem your blessings with thankfulness so they don't unravel.

– Author Unknown

I find that the more willing I am to be grateful for the small things in life, the bigger stuff just seems to show up from unexpected sources, and I am constantly looking forward to each day with all the surprises that keep coming my way!

– Louise L. Hay

Give thanks for a little and you will find a lot.

– The Hausa of Nigeria

Make it a habit to tell people thank you. To express your appreciation, sincerely and without the expectation of anything in return. Truly appreciate those around you, and you'll soon find many others around you. Truly appreciate life, and you'll find that you have more of it.

– Ralph Marston

Every time we remember to say "thank you", we experience nothing less than heaven on earth.

– Sarah Ban Breathnach

Feeling gratitude and not expressing it is like wrapping a present and not giving it."

– William Arthur Ward

Thankfulness is the beginning of gratitude. Gratitude is the completion of thankfulness. Thankfulness may consist merely of words. Gratitude is shown in acts.

– David O. McKay

Gratitude makes sense of our past, brings peace for today, and creates a vision for tomorrow.

– Melody Beattie

None is more impoverished than the one who has no gratitude. Gratitude is a currency that we can mint for ourselves, and spend without fear of bankruptcy."

– Fred De Witt Van Amburgh

No duty is more urgent than that of returning thanks.

– James Allen

FUNDRAISING READING LIST

People often ask me what great donor relations books they should read to help them in their positions in fundraising and donor relations. When I lived in New York, I used to read a book or two a week during my commute so I have some thoughts here. I can never point them to a definitive donor relations text, great ones just don't exist...yet. But I can give you a great reading list that will help you greatly in your career in non-profit work. In reading these books I have found so much that applies to my daily life and my work life that I want to share them here with you. I don't get any royalties here so just enjoy them!

CRUCIAL CONVERSATIONS
Kerry Patterson, Joseph Grenny, Ron McMillan, and Al Switzler

This book is a must-read for anyone who works with people. Since that's 99.9% of us, so that means you! I think so many of us have never been taught how to have difficult yet important conversations with people, our teammates, supervisors, etc. This book really helped me and I have attended some of their workshops and they were fabulous, as well.

LEAN IN
Sheryl Sandberg

I don't care about your politics or your thoughts about the author, but everyone, especially women in the fundraising world, should read this book. It has great points on mentoring, commitment, picking your battles, and other topics that I just keep rereading over and over. It's my book of the year and just brilliant.

GIVE AND TAKE
Adam M. Grant

I just finished this book and boy did it help me a great deal to further understand some complicated relationships I have with people. Basically, it's about how some people are givers and some are takers, but by far, the givers are both the least and most successful people in the world. Many life and work lessons here and a great read about philanthropy, too.

FISH!
Stephen C. Lundin, Harry Paul, John Christensen, Ken Blanchard

My first Vice President Cynthia Wood had our entire division read this wonderful little 100 page book. It helped change the culture of our internal workings and really some back office/ front office dynamics that weren't that healthy. A great read for a group or retreat.

STRENGTHS FINDER 2.0
Tom Rath

Another great read for a group activity or retreat, my good friend and mentor Denise Howard suggested this book to help more concretely assess my strengths...and it delivered. I learned a great deal about myself and others through learning my strengths. A great idea is to map your team's strengths so you know who to go to for specific projects and their working styles.

A SIMPLE ACT OF GRATITUDE: HOW LEARNING TO SAY THANK YOU CHANGED MY LIFE
John Kralik

I have mentioned many times on my blog, but Judge John Kralik's book on how writing 365 thank you notes changed his life is a phenomenal read and one especially powerful for those in fundraising and non-profit work.

DELIVERING HAPPINESS
Tony Hsieh

This book, written by the folks at Zappos is about customer service based culture and can truly be transformational for office culture and dynamics.

MORE GREAT READS

THINKING FAST AND SLOW
Daniel Kahneman

LAWS OF SIMPLICITY
John Maeda

THE GRATITUDE FACTOR: ENHANCING YOUR LIFE THROUGH GRATEFUL LIVING
Charles M. Shelton, PhD

WITH GRATITUDE
Jennifer Richwine

PURPLE COW
Seth Godin

THE 4 PILLARS OF DONOR RELATIONS
Lynne Wester :)

ABOUT THE AUTHOR

Lynne Wester is founder and owner of Donor Relations Guru. Using her expertise and hands-on approach, Lynne works with many high profile universities and organizations to help them keep their focus donor driven, technology savvy, strategic, and always with a splash of good humor.

Lynne is a frequent conference speaker and well-known resource for donor relations and fundraising expertise. She has been featured in *The Washington Post, CURRENTS Magazine, The Chronicle of Philanthropy* and other industry publications. She has also authored the book *The 4 Pillars of Donor Relations.*

Lynne received her undergraduate degrees from the University of South Carolina and is a loyal Gamecock alumna, donor, and fan, and holds a master's in strategic fundraising and philanthropy.

WORK WITH LYNNE

If you are interested in working with Lynne or having her speak at your next conference, you can contact her via any of the following:

WEBSITE   www.DonorRelationsGuru.com
EMAIL   Lynne@DonorRelationsGuru.com
TWITTER   @DonorGuru

ABOUT THE CONTRIBUTOR

Debbie Meyers currently serves as the Senior Director of Stewardship at University of Maryland. She has worked in advancement for more than 25 years, much of that time in higher education. In addition to creating and enhancing donor relations and stewardship programs at the University of Florida and Carnegie Mellon University, she has built communications and development programs for a Catholic high school, an art museum and a health science center development office.

As a founding board member of the Association of Donor Relations Professionals and faculty star recipient from the Council for Advancement and Support of Education, she has chaired ADRP's international conference, served on many of its committees and is a frequent, popular presenter at conferences. She also guests blogs on donor relations topics.

39159016R00188

Printed in Great Britain
by Amazon